FRONT BOOK COVER

As I was choosing the background scene for the title of this book, I loved the shades of blue but I was uncertain about the rough-looking surface that it displayed. Would it accurately portray the manuscript? As I studied the light streaming through the darkness, I sensed God gently whispering in my spirit…

In our dark, rough, and messed up world, God shines His light through the darkness and assigns those who are obedient to His call, to divinely meet with that person who needs to be touched by His love.

That's what God has been doing in my life for over 50 years, and the stories in this book are evidence of what He has accomplished through me.

JESUS, I've known from the very beginning that this is not my book. It's all yours! You had this book planned long before I even thought it was possible, and you led me to do what looked impossible. Thank you for allowing me to partner with you as you wrote each word... through me.

I dedicate this book to you, and look forward to watching how you are going to bless it and bring praise to your holy name.

DIVINE LOVE

on

ASSIGNMENT

DIVINE LOVE

on

ASSIGNMENT

Real Life Stories
of Divine Appointments
Orchestrated by God

Karen LaCount Korthase

Published by

Parakletos Press

Lake Stevens, WA

Publisher's email: DivineLoveOnAssignment@gmail.com

Copyright Use and Public Information

Unless otherwise noted, images have been used according to public information laws.

ISBN: **978-0-578-91744-3** Paperback

Limits of Liability and Disclaimer of Warranty

The author and publisher shall not be liable for the reader's misuse of this material. This book is for strictly informational and educational purposes.

Scriptures marked NLT are taken from the HOLY BIBLE, NEW LIVING TRANSLATION (NLT): Scriptures taken from the HOLY BIBLE, NEW LIVING TRANSLATION, Copyright© 1996, 2004, 2007 by Tyndale House Foundation. Used by permission of Tyndale House Publishers, Inc., Carol Stream, Illinois 60188. All rights reserved. Used by permission. Scriptures marked NKJV are taken from the NEW KING JAMES VERSION (NKJV): Scripture taken from the NEW KING JAMES VERSION®. Copyright© 1982 by Thomas Nelson, Inc. Used by permission. All rights reserved. Scriptures marked NIV are taken from the NEW INTERNATIONAL VERSION (NIV): Scripture taken from THE HOLY BIBLE, NEW INTERNATIONAL VERSION ®. Copyright© 1973, 1978, 1984, 2011 by Biblica, Inc.™. Used by permission of Zondervan. The New Testament in Modern English by J.B Phillips copyright © 1960, 1972 J. B. Phillips. Administered by The Archbishops' Council of the Church of England. Used by Permission.

Disclaimer

The views expressed are those of the author and do not reflect the official policy or position of the publisher or Parakletos Press. This publication is designed to provide accurate and authoritative information regarding the subject matter covered. It is sold with the understanding that the publisher is not engaged in rendering legal, accounting, clinical or other professional advice. If legal advice or other expert assistance is required, the services of a competent professional should be sought. The opinions expressed by the authors in this book are not endorsed by Customer Strategy Academy, and are the sole responsibility of the author rendering the opinion.

PARAKLETOS PRESS

(Greek meaning of Parakletos: Holy Spirit)

*"Never let your brotherly love fail,
nor refuse to extend your hospitality to
strangers—sometimes men have
entertained angels unawares."*
Hebrews 13:2 Phillips

ENDORSEMENTS

DIVINE LOVE ON ASSIGNMENT is a reflection of Karen's passion for Christ and how she has followed Him wholeheartedly through the years. I'm certain that people will identify with her inner dialogue of doubt and questioning. It's this inner conflict that will challenge the reader to continue reading every word! I believe God's anointing is upon this book. He will use it to move the reader to take deeper steps of faith, and trust God for miracles. These stories are powerful and SPIRIT-LED.

SUSIE BERNER – Professional Christian Fundraising Coach, Writer and Speaker

You will be inspired and buoyed by how the Love of Jesus flows through Karen to touch the lives of everyday, ordinary people in holy and extraordinary ways. Each story of her God-led encounters, which she shares both humbly and humorously, will bring a smile to your heart and encouragement to your soul. I know I'm listening more attentively for God's holy nudges to share His Divine love wherever I go!

MARILYN VANCIL – Author of "<u>Self to Lose, Self to Find</u>: Using the Enneagram to Uncover your True, God-Gifted Self"

I am pleased to recommend DIVINE LOVE ON ASSIGNMENT. In her book, Karen offers amazing everyday stories of how the Holy Spirit can produce orchestrated encounters with people. These accounts invite us to be available to "Holy Spirit Opportunities" that often come in the form of personal inconveniences or just normal everyday living. I know this book will encourage and challenge personal growth so that you can become all God created you to be.

PASTOR FRED DONALDSON – Senior Pastor of Desert Chapel, Palm Springs, CA.

Karen uses the simplicity of real-life stories to help us understand the depth of God's love for each of us. These divine encounters with strangers give us hope and confidence that God is indeed alive in us if we put our full faith in Him. I know Karen to be a woman of prayer and care, how grateful I am for this gift in writing that she shares with us. This book is empowering!

SUSAN HUTCHISON – Seattle TV News Anchor (CBS affiliate); WA. State GOP Chairman Emeritus; Former Chair, Young Life Board; and sought-after Speaker.

This book features a vivid recounting of true and powerful incidents that begin as commonplace everyday events, and end up as miraculous experiences. It is a moving example of how by faithfully obeying the prompting of the Holy Spirit, we can realize God's unforeseen yet perfect plan in what otherwise is viewed as dire and hopeless situations. It is not unlike how a routine boat ride on Lake Galilee 2000 years ago, turned in to a life changing walk on water. Be prepared to be elevated from the ordinary to the supernatural. This is a highly recommended and inspiring read!

TIM MALKE – President, Middle East Gospel Outreach, Upland, CA.

ACKNOWLEDGEMENTS

MY HUSBAND: Craig, even before I began writing this book, you were the one who kept encouraging me to begin, by saying, "Karen, this book will be a blessing to others, and it needs to be written." Your support, motivation, and being my all-around cheerleader was amazing! And even when I told you the publishing costs, or the fact that I wanted to give the proceeds away to a charity, you continued to walk through this laborious journey with me. Your technical help and spiritual guidance were indispensable. Thank you for never giving up on the dream God placed in my heart.

KARIN MELVARD: My precious friend, when God chose you to help me with this book, the weight on my shoulders was lifted! He knew I needed your giftings and grace to keep me focused and walk with me on this journey. You stood by me through each issue we faced and have been an absolute blessing to me. I am deeply indebted to you.

FERVENT FIVE: My closest prayer support team—Jo Stewart, Linda Skinner, Ruthmarie Schroeder and Karin Melvard were invaluable. When God brought us together, I had no idea what a blessing and support you would be to me. Whenever I texted a prayer need, you went immediately to prayer. You are all a gift from God. Recently, Sunny Hancock and Susan Lyneis joined us and now we are the *Fervent Seven*. Although they were not part of this prayer group during this writing, they certainly stood beside me in prayer in the same way.

MY FAMILY: In the beginning, the only reason I compiled these stories was because I thought someday my grandsons may read them. Little did I know what God had planned. Thank you for holding me up in prayer and believing that God could use even me to write a book.

PRECIOUS FRIENDS: Through the years, God has placed several pivotal people in my life who had an important effect on the writing of this book. You know who you are! I don't dare try to acknowledge you all or I would be sure to miss someone. However, I do need to mention my precious sister-in-law, Mara Brodeur. She encouraged, pushed, begged and prayed like crazy for me to get these stories told. You all trusted that God had a purpose in asking me to take on this insurmountable task. May you be blessed for your faithfulness in prayer for me.

JOANN YOUNGQUIST: You are my niece, but we grew up like sisters. Early on, when I shared my unusual stories, you were the one responsible for nudging me to record them. There never would have been a book if I hadn't listened to your encouragement.

CONTENTS

INTRODUCTION

The words lifted off the page and entered my spirit.

For years my husband encouraged me to record the unusual experiences I had with strangers. My response was always the same. "I'm not a writer!" Besides, I knew I would never write a book. However, I decided I should at least record them to hand down to my family. As a result, years of accumulated stories poured into the Word file of my computer.

In the beginning, I could not understand why strangers would continually begin conversations with me when I was out and about. In time, I finally realized God was responsible for orchestrating each contact. When I shared these unusual experiences with my husband, he would always say, "I think you wear an invisible sign that reads: *Tell me your life story...I love to listen.*"

Tell me your life story... I love to listen.

I never had a desire to have a ministry that involved strangers. However, I was amazed how God gave me the boldness and compassion to graciously respond to them. It was *amazing* to experience.

Years later, as the stories continued to accumulate, I sensed a gentle whisper saying, *compile them.* Due to my own insecurities with writing, I ignored the thought.

It wasn't until *much* later that I asked God's forgiveness for not obeying His original plan for me. I decided that I should at least explore what He might have in mind. So, I prayed, "Lord, you know I'm not a writer, but if you feel these stories can bless others, show me how to communicate them in writing. I need *You* to literally write them through me, because it feels impossible to even begin."

In 2018, I had the best of intentions as I tried to compile them. I became overwhelmed and put it aside. The longer I waited, the more impossible it seemed.

A year later, I thought, *if I don't get serious about this project, I will be too old to accomplish it.* Once again, I prayed, "Lord, I need a clear word from You, if compiling these stories is really Y*our* plan."

My husband and I had been reading through the New Testament together. On September 5th, 2019, it was my turn to read 2 Corinthians 8 NKJV, aloud. When I came to verses 10-12, it was like the words lifted off the page and landed in my spirit!

Introduction

Tears began to fall uncontrollably as I sensed God had clearly spoken to me. My husband reread the three verses to see if *he* understood what I was seeing. He began…

> *"And in this I give advice: It is to your advantage not only to be doing what you began and were desiring to do a year ago, but now you also must complete the doing of it, that as there was a readiness to desire it, so there also may be a completion out of what you have. For if there is first a willing mind, it is accepted according to what one has, and not according to what he does not have."*

I can't tell you how many times I had said, "I'm a storyteller, **not** a writer!" But to me, verse 12 said that it is *not according to what (abilities) I don't think I have*. I was even amazed how it mentioned *what I began and desired to do a year ago.* I had started by editing former stories I had recorded, but with so many distractions, I stopped writing. The scripture went on to say how I must *complete the doing of it!* I was shocked! Now, I felt certain that God had given me a clear word.

Could it be any clearer? Some might say I took scripture out of context. I didn't care. I knew God had given me a personal word and stirred my spirit to get serious about bringing these true stories to completion.

And, if He called me to do it, I knew He would equip me! Boldly, I made a mental declaration:

Lord Jesus, **I CAN'T...but...YOU CAN***...through me!*

As I began to write, a joy rose inside my spirit. However, shortly after I had started writing, unusual things happened to my computer. My curser would jump around, or I would suddenly lose large quantities of paragraphs that I had just written.

If it wasn't my computer having issues, it was my printer. My husband helped me solve one problem after another. I found myself spending more time trying to solve technical problems than actually writing.

However, when I began to have one health issue after another, I finally realized what was going on. The enemy of my soul did not want this manuscript written; and at different points in the writing, I sensed a voice saying, "You *can't* write this book. No one will want to read it!"

I knew it wasn't the Lord's voice because He wouldn't bring fear in my heart. So, my husband and I began coming against the enemy and his crafty schemes through prayer, in the name of Jesus.

Even in the midst of these difficulties, I felt *compelled* to write; I spent hours each day writing, editing, and re-editing. It was like I couldn't keep up with the thoughts *God* was giving me.

I couldn't have written this manuscript without my husband's encouragement and prayer support. Several times I wanted to stop writing, but between him and several prayer warrior friends, they would *not* let me give up. They literally carried me in prayer as I went through major spiritual warfare.

I asked a publisher if these issues happened to any of her other Christian writers. She immediately said, "All the time!" As I continued to yield to God, I was certain He would win.

Then, one day I clearly realized: THIS IS NOT MY BOOK. IT'S ALL HIS!

In fact, God clearly showed me that all proceeds will be donated. I am sensing it will go to a ministry where children are taken out of human trafficking.

May God be glorified!

TO THE READER

This book is filled with Divine Appointments that God has brought to me for over 50 years. As you read, I hope you will take the time to ponder each story. Ask God to show you what He wants you to personally take away from what you've read.

And lastly, would you join me in taking a moment to pray for the person that lived this story. I may have planted a spiritual seed in his/her heart but the seed needs to be watered through prayer.

As you read, keep in mind that God gives us a free will in how we respond to others. You may think, *God had better not ask me to talk to strangers like Karen does.*

Remember, God always gives us a choice. For me, the longer I love and serve Him, the more I want my life to line up with His plan for me.

There are occasional scriptures placed throughout some of these stories. If you go to the back of the book, you will see that they have been recorded in more detail on the SCRIPTURE REFERENCES page.

My desire is that you will be blessed by each story I have shared.

Karen

I believe God wants to use us as ministers

of encouragement and blessing to others,

in even the smallest of situations.

WHERE MY STORY BEGINS

Without realizing it, I was mentored
by a very wise woman.

Since I was in my early 20s, I began having unusual encounters with people, mostly strangers. When it first started, I questioned why. In time, it became clear that the Lord had brought each of these people into my life.

I began to see a pattern.

When I was flying on an airplane, grocery shopping, or in other ordinary places, strangers would come up to me and begin conversations. Then, when they finished, they'd often say, "I can't believe I just told you that story about myself. I've never told it to anyone."

My husband says I wear an invisible sign that reads...*Tell me your life story, I love to listen.*

I can't say I always love to listen *because* I'm often in a hurry. However, when one of these experiences takes place, the Lord gives me *His* grace to be patient and allow *Him* to use me how *He* chooses.

I'm often asked where I get my boldness to respond to strangers. Some think it's my personality. Not a chance! If

I had *not* witnessed my mother, who always talked with strangers, I doubt I would have ever done the same. Let me explain…

When I was young, I often wondered why God placed me in the family He did. My dad was 50 and mother was 44, when I was born. As I grew up, I wasn't only embarrassed by my mother's age but also her weight. She was quite heavy, wore an old-fashioned hairstyle and no make-up. However, strangers seemed to look beyond her outward appearance. She carried a confidence in everything she said and did. When she spoke, people listened.

I went everywhere with mother. From birth to leaving for college, she dragged me along to jails, prisons and nursing homes where she ministered to inmates and the elderly.

In high school, I would take my violin to play at places where she ministered. It wasn't until later, I realized those experiences were training me to deal with strangers more effectively, for *my* future ministry.

Mother was a great storyteller, diligent prayer-warrior, Christian Women's speaker, and had a deep love for the Lord. Her boldness and concern for others had an amazing impact on my life. It wasn't until I was in my mid-twenties that I thanked the Lord for choosing *my* specific parents to raise me. He knew the exact home where I needed to be placed.

I don't remember ever seeing my mother fearful in any situation. She only saw *opportunities* to be available for God. She always reached out to others when she felt impressed by the Holy Spirit.

One such experience took place in the early 1930's, many years before I was conceived. She was driving home after grocery shopping. As she drove over the railroad-tracks, she saw a small house just a short distance away, and sensed the Lord was telling her to stop there, even though she had no idea who lived in the home.

Mother had learned not to question these promptings because she had experienced God's faithfulness each time she listened. When she reached the house, she walked up the stairs to the porch and knocked on the door. A woman's voice was crying loudly with intermittent groans. She knew it was serious so she tried the door knob. It was unlocked and she walked inside to see a delirious-looking woman who was standing in a bedroom, holding her baby. "My baby, my baby is dead, my baby is dead!"

Mother lovingly comforted the young woman and gently pried the baby away from the mother's arms. After checking the baby girl, she gently placed her in the cradle. Her skin was cold and greyish in color and my mother knew this precious baby was in the arms of Jesus. Then, she covered the baby from head to toe and turned to the grieving mother.

Slowly, as she walked the mother to the living-room sofa, fearing the woman might collapse on the floor, she helped her to the sofa. Then, she turned to face the young mother. She wrapped her arms around her and gently rocked her back and forth like a child who needed to be quieted from some unexplained fear. She continued holding her until the woman's sobbing was calmed and the trembling had subdued. Gradually, the woman was able to speak and the husband was called.

My mother could have ignored the prompting of the Holy Spirit. Instead, she fearlessly walked into that woman's life, comforted her and prayed for her in her desperate time of need. She continued to reach out to the young mother and in a short time, after that first encounter, mother led her to invite Jesus into her heart and life. Hope was restored, and eventually God gave her another baby girl to take the place of the one He had called to heaven.

This story has taught me that...

I, too, want to be sensitive to the voice of the Holy Spirit and be obedient to what He calls me to do.

Now I look back and recognize her influence on my life. I've dealt with many of the same kinds of situations as she did, including her experiences with homeless people who stopped by our farmhouse near the freeway. They would leave after a shower, hair-cut, wearing dad's clean clothes, and a full meal; the entire time they would hear about Jesus.

In every experience God brought into my mother's life, she was always faithful to share God's Love and would leave the person with Hope. I grew up thinking that all Christians (followers of Jesus) had these experiences. I soon learned this simply wasn't true.

In time, someone labeled my continued encounter with strangers as *Divine Appointments*.

There were times when I thought they should be called *Divine Interruptions* because they didn't always happen when it was convenient. However, they definitely **are** Divine because God is always the one who orchestrates the details of placing them in my life. Each time, He gives me words of encouragement and hope to share with the ones He brings.

I don't understand why He has called me to a ministry with mostly strangers. Like my mother, the people He brings into my life are often messed up, hurting, and need the Savior's love.

However, they always teach me something about myself, and the greatness of my Lord. He uses them to humble and teach me that the *only* way I can deal with these situations is when I surrender everything to Him: my time… my words… my life.

I not only need to be available at all times, I also need to be spiritually prepared. We don't always get to choose how God uses us if we are open to His leading.

Ministering to strangers, would never have been something I would have chosen. However, obeying what He asks of me always means applying the scripture, *Love thy neighbor as thyself.*

Who is our neighbor? Any person with whom we come in contact as we walk through our day; whether that person is a professional or a street person. Whoever He brings, it doesn't matter how much status or wealth they have or don't have. We are all sinners, in need of a Savior.

When GOD brings Divine Appointments to us, it means He trusts us to show His Love, and to share the Hope they can have when they surrender their life to Jesus.

CROCKPOT

God began over twenty years ago,
trying to get his attention.

I'd had a busy day filled with errands but needed a few groceries before I headed home to start dinner. I knew Craig was on his way home from work, so I rushed through the store, stopping at the meat section last.

Since Craig's cancer diagnosis, I had become more specific as to what type of meat to buy. I needed assistance, so I was delighted to see the butcher unloading his tall cart.

"Excuse me sir," I politely called. His back was facing me but I continued, "Do you have any organic ground beef?"

He turned around and with a smile, pointed to his cart. "This is what you want! It has no hormones, antibiotics or steroids and was grass-fed since it was young."

I was grateful to learn that my favorite grocery store now carried quality organic meat. So, I asked for 3 one-pound packages of hamburger. After he filled the order, I thanked him and turned away. He promptly queried, "Do you need any steaks or roasts? They come from the same company with the same quality. This is a new line we carry."

Had I replied, "No thank you," this experience would have never happened.

Instead, I chose a roast and said, "How would you prepare this? I'd like to use my crockpot." After the words fell out of my mouth, I thought: *That's crazy, why did I ask that question? I've fixed many roasts in my crockpot.*

The butcher anxiously shared how he would prepare the meat, but added. "I can't use a crockpot anymore because my ex-wife took it with her when we divorced."

What I said next surprised me even more, but without a blink, I responded; "Now why would she ever divorce a kind man like you?"

He had a surprised look and said, "You really think so?" I guess when I made that comment, it made him feel valued.

Before I knew it, he started telling me about his life!

As he continued to talk, it literally felt like God had orchestrated that moment for His purpose. No one could hear us because no one was coming near the meat department. It was very surreal, as though an invisible circle of protection was drawn around us. The store was very busy with shoppers but absolutely *no one* passed by.

The man must have sensed the privacy and felt a trust to begin speaking so freely. Perhaps my mature age caused him to feel safe to share his thoughts. No matter, I listened and focused on every word he spoke, even though I had been in a rush to get home. I know that God did that for me.

After sharing a few things about his divorce, his brother, and his 19-year-old son, he hesitated a moment and said, "I want to share something I have only told one other person. I *can't* believe I'm telling you this, but years ago, I went fishing all alone on a river where the nearest town was 12 miles away. The weather turned unexpectedly cold, and I was not prepared. In a short time, my feet began to feel extremely cold."

At this point, I wanted to ask him why he hadn't left before he froze to death, but I kept silent.

He continued, "I only had one pair of white cotton socks that I wore in my wading boots. I realized I was in trouble because my feet began to feel like they were nearing frost bite. I was so cold I didn't know what to do so I began to talk to God. Now, that was *not* something I normally did but I was desperate."

My ears perked up even more.

He went on, "I told Him I needed *warmer* socks. I don't know why I asked for that specific of a request because how was God going to give me socks with no one else around? Then, as I turned around and looked ahead of me, on the ground was something red and rolled into a ball. I picked it up and as I unfolded it, I was holding a pair of red wool socks with grey stripes! The amazing thing was that they felt like they had been warmed in an oven! There was no logical explanation that those socks could be sitting there when I hadn't seen them before. And I certainly couldn't explain how they could be warm when it was only 36 degrees. I quickly put them on and was overwhelmed with amazement. Had God really heard my prayer? I just couldn't explain it any other way."

Customers continued to remain outside of this invisible wall that God had drawn around us.

He then conveyed, "Sometime later, as I was standing in the water, preparing to hook my next fish, I was still thinking about my unexpected answer to prayer when my fishing pliers which I'd used for a brief moment, suddenly slipped out of my hand into the water! I couldn't believe I had been so careless! I did my best to try to find them but the water was too deep."

My curiosity was piqued to find out the rest of the story.

"Moments later, I thought, if God can provide socks, maybe I could ask him to help me find my blue-handled pliers," he expressed. "As I headed to the shore, out of the corner of my eye, I saw something shiny in the shallow water's edge. I reached down and picked it up. It was a pair of red-handled pliers that were a familiar brand name and I knew were far more valuable than the ones I had lost! By this time, I was really in shock!"

He concluded, "When I thought of the events that had taken place that day, I knew I could never share them with anyone else because *no one* would ever believe my story."

I calmly looked in his eyes and said, "I know why that experience happened to you."

His eyebrows raised and his eyes opened wide as he waited for the answer.

"God began over twenty years ago trying to get your attention because He loves you so much," I explained.

When he heard the word *God*, he connected it with church and promptly told me how he had gone to church with his brother, but he couldn't figure out some of the things they were talking about.

I then said, "Well, it's like walking up to a stranger's mailbox and opening his mail. If you opened any personal letters, you may not understand the context within that letter because you wouldn't have a relationship with that person. The same is true with God. The things you hear in church, or read in the Bible may not be understandable because you don't have a relationship with Him."

I emphasized once again, "I believe God has been speaking to you in a number of different situations, wanting you to know how much He loves you and wanting a relationship with you."

His response was, "But I don't know if God could ever forgive me for some of the bad things I've done."

"I can assure you," I responded, "God *will* forgive you of absolutely *anything*, if you just ask Him." Then I became very serious and gently said, "Have you ever asked Jesus to forgive you of your sins and asked Him to come into your heart and life?"

He lowered his head and softly said, "No...I don't think so." I was actually shocked at myself because I don't tend to ask a perfect stranger that question.

Suddenly, I began to sense that people were now entering God's protective shield around us and I no longer felt the freedom to continue the conversation.

So I said, "I need to get home and you need to get back to work, but I want to ask one quick question before I leave and you don't need to answer. But I want you to think about it." I continued, "If you were to die today, do you know where you'd spend eternity?" There was no hesitation at all. He looked at me and once again responded softly, "I really don't know."

Crockpot

I longed to continue the conversation and explain how he could know for certain, but I realized the boss may walk by, so I asked if he would like to continue the conversation next time I came into the store.

"I probably won't be here because it's my brother who is a butcher here and he needed some help, so I came to work with him today. I actually work at a different store as a butcher. If you come back here and talk with him, he looks a lot like me and you may think it's me, but I probably will not be here. My name is Tim and my brother's name is Jim," he explained.

I was grateful to finally put a name with his face. We had been so busy talking, we hadn't introduced ourselves.

I quickly reached into my purse and pulled out a scrap piece of paper and wrote my e-mail address down. I thought, *"What am I doing giving out my e-mail to a stranger?*

In a joking but kind way, I said, "Don't you ever share this info with anyone else." Then I said, "Tim, I don't want you to feel obligated to contact me, but if you want to know more about why God has been trying to get your attention and what He wants to do in your life, then feel free to contact me." (And in case he did, I knew I had a number of different men who would be willing to meet with him. I felt all I could do was plant the seed.)

Before we said goodbye, I said, "You know Tim, you may think you were here because your brother asked for your help, but God placed you in this store today and had you standing by that section of meats. Then, He brought *me* here to ask you my meat question, all because He wanted you to hear one more time how much He loves you."

Tim stood quietly with misty eyes but with a look of hope. He smiled and we said goodbye. However, I couldn't move for a few moments. Gentle tears of joy filled my eyes and I felt like I was standing on holy ground. God's presence lingered with me as people began to enter the protected area. I realized it was the question about the crockpot that God used to open the conversation.

I think of the years when I would have been hesitant to share God's truth with an absolute stranger. I would have thought, *it's none of my business to get involved in that person's life.* Oh, I have missed so many opportunities.

It is amazing to be sensitive to the Holy Spirit's leading. And when these situations open up, they leave me with an unbelievable sense of JOY!

MY SIXTH GRADE ANGEL

My heart ached for her because she
desperately wanted to be chosen.

It was my first year as a teacher and I was responsible for the music program in grades kindergarten through sixth grade.

As a teacher, it's *easy* to pick a favorite student, even though one shouldn't show it. A particular girl in 6th grade was *not* one I would have easily picked. I had no idea how God would use me in this girl's life and in turn, how she would be used to teach me a valuable lesson.

Sherry looked older than other students. She sat in the back row and looked anything but cheerful and alert. She was overweight, wore an un-kempt hairstyle and had buck teeth.

When she tried talking, it was extremely difficult to understand her garbled words. She sat in a wheelchair and pecked with a bent finger on an electric typewriter because she couldn't write with a pencil. I was told she was considered to be spastic, but the official diagnosis was Cerebral Palsy.

In the beginning of my relationship with her, I felt great pity and concern, but questioned why she had been placed in a normal classroom and not one that would be more suitable for her physical needs.

I was very conscious not to give her special attention; this is how she wanted it. However, I found myself wanting to reach out and pad the walls of limitations around her. There was so little she could do. Even though her words sounded choked as they stumbled spasmodically from her lips, she was determined to learn how to sing.

Some months after our first meeting, I began planning a Fifth & Sixth Grade Spring Concert. The children were all given an opportunity to audition. To make the selection, I had each student come into my office, sing a familiar tune, then I would give them my decision.

Even though their voices were still underdeveloped, if they could carry a tune, they were chosen.

Thankfully, the ones who couldn't carry a tune *didn't* try out…except for one! It was Sherry, my 6th grade wheelchair student!

How could I allow a child to sing in this select choir when she could only sing off-key?

I was in a dilemma. My heart ached for her because she desperately wanted to be chosen.

I had watched her many times in the classroom when she got excited or nervous. Her body would stiffen and, as her voice began squealing odd sounds, there were no understandable words. The more she tried, the more frustrated she'd get and the more drool would slide over her lips.

When it came time to invite Sherry to my office, I prayed, "Lord, how will I tell her she can't be chosen? Please give me wisdom and show me how to help her feel valued."

This choir was very important to her but how could I be truthful and let her know her voice wasn't suitable for any type of musical performance?

While I was still figuring out how to handle this dilemma, words came spilling out, "Sherry, we're going to work together on this because I want you to be in the choir."

Shocked, I promptly thought: Am I crazy? Then I continued. "It's going to take some work because, as you know, when your body gets excited, your voice sings something different than you intend. We need to have a plan and I've got an idea."

I hesitated for a moment and thought, *where did that come from?*

Here I was getting ready to graciously tell her she couldn't be in the choir and then those words came out of my mouth?! Clearly, the Lord had taken over and I was grateful because I could have really damaged this young girl's emotions.

I continued explaining to her in detail, how she first needed to learn how to calm her body by slowly taking in a deep breath through her nose and then slowly & quietly letting it flow through her pursed lips. We talked about how she could keep her muscles relaxed and then softly let the music come out. However, my mind was in conflict: *How is this even possible for her?*

Then, God gave me another idea! I asked if her mother owned a record player. They did have one, so I told her to have mom play a song with which she could sing along. Then, I ended with, "Let me know when you're satisfied with your practice & we'll schedule an appointment for you to sing for me."

Suddenly, as she tried to speak, her body stiffened and she got very excited. I was concerned she might slide out of her wheelchair. She was trying to tell me something *really* important.

It took me some time to finally understand she was trying to tell me she didn't want to wait! She was inviting me to her home for dinner the following week and she explained how she would practice all week and then sing for me when I came for dinner!

I accepted her invitation and then thought, *what did I just get myself into?* I had to follow through because the least I could do was be gracious enough to meet with her where she felt most comfortable, in her own home.

The following week as I drove to her address, I realized she lived in a really poor area of town. The tiny house and yard desperately needed work. I went to the door and met the single mom who was caring for Sherry's demanding needs, and also a younger sister. As I looked around the small room, the furniture was sparse and the floor was a worn dark green & black linoleum. There was no table where we could sit to eat so they asked me to sit on the sofa in the small living room.

As I sat down, I felt the springs of the sofa beneath me. However, as sad as the furnishings looked, the tiny home was sparkling clean.

Within moments, a small tray of food was brought to the living room by the mother. There were four plain hot-dogs and a small bowl of plain red Jell-O, just enough to serve each of us one small serving, but no extra.

I had brought home-baked cookies for dessert and the girls were delighted! I knew this simple meal wasn't the real reason I was there.

The meal seemed rushed with limited conversation. I was still chewing my food when Sherry squealed, "Can I sing for you?" I couldn't understand her garbled words, so her mother interpreted, and I responded, "I would love to hear your song."

Her mother placed Sherry's wheelchair in the middle of the small living room and walked over to turn on the old record player.

As the music started, Sherry was both *nervous* and *excited*. The combination of these two emotions didn't work well, because it caused her body to stiffen.

The sounds from her voice *didn't* match the music being played and she began to look panicked. Tears began to fall. Her mother quickly turned off the record player.

She sat still and her voice was silent, but welled-up tears began to trickle down her face.

I quickly walked over and knelt in front of her, gently and slowly saying, "Sherry, I know you can do this. Now take a deep breath and quiet your body."

I waited as she went through the 'getting-relaxed' motions, then I continued, "When the music starts, sing softly. You watch…beautiful music will come out."

Her mother looked concerned as to whether her daughter would be able to master this difficult feat. However, at my cue, she started the music once again.

I got down next to the wheelchair, coaching her with breathing and relaxation techniques, until the words and music started flowing softly from her voice! I clearly had to fight back the tears as I continued to nod my head to the music and give her expressions of acceptance, with a big smile.

When the music stopped, mother, sister and I broke out in a loud applause, simultaneously yelling, "Woo-hoo!" She had passed the test!

I cupped my hands around her crippled hands, slowly and gently saying, "Sherry, I would be proud to have you in our choir!"

She began crying loudly with a groaning sound, as her body stiffened again. This time it was tears of joy! I hugged her and was certain the Lord had helped her to sing because He loved her even more than I did.

After that evening in her home, I would often hear a gentle knock at my office door and there would be Sherry sitting in her wheel chair. She waited for an invitation to be invited into my small office. Her excuse was that she wanted to practice the choir music with me.

At this point, I no longer saw her outward appearance; I now saw her precious heart as I grew to love her. I realized she was really no different than any other child. She was very bright, but was locked in a body she couldn't control.

May finally arrived – time for the Spring Choir Performance. I wondered what would happen with Sherry.

At 7 pm sharp, the children filed into the auditorium and found their places on the choir risers. Sherry was last & was wheeled in by one of the boys to the left, at the end of the front row. She was wearing her best dress and shoes that looked like hand-me-downs but her face *absolutely glowed*.

Without the audience seeing, I gave her some positive facial expressions and encouraged her to take a deep breath to relax her body. She followed my directions and gave me her precious crooked smile.

When the music started, I kept a peripheral view of what she was doing and occasionally placed my finger over my mouth to encourage her to sing softly. The performance went well and my heart was so grateful with what the Lord had accomplished in Sherry.

When the concert was over and the students returned to their classroom, *they* told Sherry for the first time how proud they were of her! That performance did more for her, and her classmates, than any of us teachers could have imagined.

Following the Spring Concert, on one of her visits to my office, her conversation turned to spiritual questions. I was surprised at the depth of her thinking and interest. I realized God had it all planned. I began to share about Jesus and His love for her, trying to make it as clear as possible to understand. She hung on every word as I explained how she could invite Him into her heart and life.

That afternoon I had the privilege of praying with her to receive Jesus as her personal Savior. When the prayer ended, it was evident the Lord had clearly transformed her spirit because she beamed as if a powerful light-bulb had been turned on! Her heart was obviously filled with His joy.

I continued to explain what faith was, why we have a Bible, and how we can talk to Jesus in prayer whenever we desire. She had faced a lot of rejection and spent so much time alone. She suddenly realized she had a new friend Who would always love and accept her and would never leave her. His name was Jesus!

I can hardly believe this amazing experience happened *so* many years ago. I remember it like it happened last week. Sadly, however, I lost contact with Sherry when I got married seven months later and moved to the East Coast.

I began a whole new life, but I *never* forgot Sherry.

As I've traveled through life, Sherry is someone whom God used to teach me a valuable life lesson: how to love a person who was shunned by most.

I had *no* idea how many opportunities I would be given in my lifetime to apply what I had learned.

I'm certain Sherry is now with Jesus because her life-expectancy was short. I'm also certain that someday I'll see her again. In heaven, she won't need a wheelchair; instead of uncontrolled sounds, she'll be praising God with all the angels – singing boldly and with clarity as she dances in worship before the Lord!

CLINIQUE DEPARTMENT

"It's like you've been sent to me!"

I had gone to the Nordstrom Anniversary pre-sale in July. And, before I go any further, I think I need to explain how I hesitate to shop at this wonderful store because it's easy to get swept into wanting more than I really need.

I hadn't been there for ages. As I walked through the store, I saw several items beckoning me. But I decided to stay focused on finding only the two items I came in to get.

I quickly made my way to the Clinique cosmetic department, looking for a specific item, when an attractive, young employee offered to help me.

I asked about a specific product for age spots. She told me she had used it for a couple of years and her 32-year-old skin was flawless. She began with sharing the information about the importance of using sunscreen. I told her I didn't use it because with my white hair, it was important to have a tan face or I'd look washed out.

She then moved to the topic of the sun's danger with regards to cancer and told me she had just had two moles removed on her skin that were pre-cancerous. I asked if those two areas had been exposed to sun and she said, "Actually, no." My response was, "Interesting."

It was at that point I said, "In my limited research, the thing I feel is even more critical than sun exposure, is what we eat and drink. I'm convinced an alkaline body is less susceptible to cancer because cancer feeds on an acidic environment."

Suddenly, she gasped and responded, "I can't believe we're having this conversation! This is so amazing. I've recently become interested in this topic because of some health issues I've been having."

I learned she had been raised in Canada and met a man from the U.S. Then, she moved to Washington State, and married him sometime later.

She also shared what her two medical issues were and I responded, "Actually, I've actually dealt with those. Matter-of-fact, after 20 years of dealing with severe fatigue, I was diagnosed with Chronic Fatigue Syndrome, which also didn't give me any answers for relief because doctors had no answers."

She asked what ended up happening? So, I shared what I had discovered and how I had been helped.

We had talked for a while and at this point, I said, "I'd better leave or you're going to either get fired for talking so long with your customer, or you're not going to make any sales."

She responded, "Don't worry about my job. I'm just so amazed with the information you are sharing with me. I feel like you have somehow been sent here to help me." Then she gave me a big hug! I was quite surprised by her response.

"It's just so amazing how I've been recently thinking about how I needed to change my diet. I recently heard someone mention the importance of an alkaline diet. Honestly, I had no idea where to begin looking or who to talk to, but here you are! It's like you've been sent to me!" she responded again.

I smiled and said, "Brie, there's something you need to know about me. These kinds of situations happen to me *all* the time. Her eyes got big as I explained more. "I actually call them, 'Divine Appointments' because I believe God plans and orchestrates them."

She responded, "Wow. This is amazing." She just couldn't get over the thought of how I had come into her department that day and she happened to be the one who assisted me because, actually, when I arrived there, it looked like she had an appointment with another person and she was not going to be able to help me. But at the last minute, her customer didn't show up, and she was available to work with me.

She didn't want to stop talking and I would have loved to continue, but I had to hurry on my way because I needed to pick up our 6-year-old grandson after his last day of Day Camp. So, when I told her I really did need to hurry on my way, she asked if she could give me her e-mail address because she wanted to stay in touch. Of course, I agreed.

Then, once again, before I left, she gave me another big hug.

She was so precious and so genuine. Somehow, I knew I'd see her again, and I knew I needed to make contact within the week.

As I walked out of the store, heading to my car, I realized I had once again experienced another amazing Divine Appointment because I felt His joy sweep over me. Already, I looked forward to seeing her again. God loved her so much that He sent her a messenger. And, I thanked Him that He was able to use an almost 70-year-old, inadequate, and weathered woman, who needed some help with her skin, so she headed to the Clinique counter.

Once again, He had answered my heart's cry to be used by Him if He promised to be there to speak through me. And He did!

LADY CHECKER at WALMART

Self-doubt can turn our God-inspired
thoughts into fabrications.

I *never plan* to get involved in a stranger's life.

However, every morning when I spend time with Jesus, I surrender my life and time to Him, to use me that day in any way He desires. I should never complain when He drops a stranger or situation right into my life, to extend His love to them, through me.

As usual, I was not choosing to make conversation with anyone at Walmart. I was anxious to get home.

Hoping for a Divine Appointment is never my plan. And actually, when He orchestrates one, I don't even realize it. Usually, it starts with a stranger who begins a conversation with me. Then, it's not until the end, when I walk away, I recognize I have just been *on assignment* for my Lord.

This time, however, was different than other experiences. I was the one who began the conversation.

I had been shopping at Walmart, and as I walked over to the check-out counter, I couldn't help but notice the customer in front of me. As she was unloading her items on the conveyor belt, I wondered what kind of life she was experiencing. She was tattered and appeared needy. She fished through her purse to find all her money. Actually, I wondered if the Lord might ask me to pay for her groceries. *That* has happened before.

As the lady dumped out a pile of loose change, I thought, *where did she get all that change?* It seemed to take forever for the checker to count her money, and the line behind us was getting longer.

After she finished counting all the coins, I noticed the checker appeared very weary.

It was my turn to buy my few items, so I decided to show kindness and said to the checker, "I'm so sorry the former customer took so much of your time and you had to count all her change."

"Oh," she responded, as she began checking my items, "That's not unusual, it happens a lot. The problem is that I'm just so tired."

She continued to check each item as she talked. "I have 3 more hours to work tonight and there are only 2 checkers in the store!"

I quickly responded, "I'm so sorry for all your stress."

"Oh, it's not your fault. The problem is that I was in the hospital for a month and I've just come back to work today."

"What?" I was in shock that she was even at work.

"Yes, I got a MRSA infection in my knee. At one point, I was concerned I might lose my whole leg! So, I lost a month of work. But when I was released, I had to return to work because I need to pay my bills. I'm absolutely exhausted!"

My heart ached for her and I wanted to stop everything right there and pray for her, but the line was long and I assumed her supervisor wouldn't appreciate my distracting her.

I took out my credit card to pay for my items and slipped my hand over hers and softly said, "I will be praying for you to have the strength to finish your shift. And, I will continue to pray for your health, as you continue to heal." I paused with a big smile and added, "By the way, I think you're doing a great job!" She thanked me over and over as I walked away.

As I headed to the front door, I saw an employee with a name tag, 'Assistant Manager.' I quickly walked over to her and asked, "Could you do me a big favor?" She looked surprised and responded, "Of course. How can I help you?"

I told the manager I wanted to give a report on one of her checkers. A frown suddenly came over her face, thinking it was going to be negative. Then, when I gave a positive report about the checker, she was shocked and so grateful.

Her response told me that too many people are quick to give complaints, but never positive reports to encourage employees, especially those working at minimum wage jobs.

The manager glowed and thanked me for sharing this report, promising me she would do something to honor this employee.

Years ago, I learned the importance of giving 'good reports' when I've been helped by an exceptional employee or one who appears that he/she needs encouragement. It's an opportunity to bless that person!

Actually, we should take every opportunity to bless as many people as we can, with positive words, every day! That even includes our family, friends, neighbors and most of all, our God! He loves hearing our praise and thankfulness.

After that encounter, I walked to my car, just sat there for a few minutes and started to review this incident in my thoughts.

I realized that before I even talked with the cashier, while standing in line, my spirit sensed I was supposed to encourage her. But I immediately started *doubting* what I thought was actually from God.

Isn't that what often happens? DOUBT can certainly turn our God-inspired thoughts into fabrications.

Think about it.

What if I was wrong and it really was just my own idea, not coming from God? Wouldn't it still be an opportunity to bless the other person?

> I believe there are a multitude of times when God's Spirit speaks to us, asking us to do something, yet we start questioning our thoughts. If we asked our self, "What if I didn't really hear from God. Would I damage this person or bless this person if I respond to what I feel I have heard?"

The other thing that creeps up is FEAR.

Thoughts enter our mind such as, *I can't talk to that person. People would think I'm crazy.* Or, *I'd come unraveled if I had to talk to a complete stranger. I don't even know what I'd say!*

I want to close this simple story with the most important thing I've learned over the years concerning Divine Appointments: **It's not about me!**

Actually, *the more frightened and insecure I am, the more God loves to take over and speak through me, if I surrender to Him and just open my mouth.*

PAY IT FORWARD

I'm amazed how a simple experience of
giving can fill one's heart with such joy.

Some years ago, my husband, Craig, was diagnosed with a rare form of cancer. It was a difficult and emotional season for both of us. Gratefully, we learned some valuable lessons:

FIRST: When his treatment came to an end, we were honestly able to say, "When we have Jesus, we have everything we need." God literally carried us through this whole experience.

*SECOND: A*s I watched Craig walk through this difficult ordeal, he continued to be conscious of how he responded to his doctors, nurses, and medical staff; he was always respectful and positive by showing an attitude of thankfulness, a grateful heart and never complained. He also had a desire to bless others, in *any* way he could.

THIRD: God used him to pray for the other patients in the Infusion Room, where his chemo-therapy was administered. Others were blessed.

The following story was how I was influenced by *his desire to bless others*. This story happened in a most simple way.

One day, I headed to a nearby shopping center that had a relatively new department store. I decided to check it out because I had heard the prices were reasonable, for the quality products they carried. I found a couple of items I liked and headed to the dressing room to try them on.

In the room next to me, I could hear a young mother with a baby in a stroller and a toddler, who obviously was not enjoying his experience in the small changing area. I tried to ignore the interaction but when I heard the mother's timid voice speaking on her cell-phone saying, "Honey, don't we even have $10 in our account so that I can buy a new Summer top? I found one for only $4 and I really need it." Her husband had obviously responded with a NO response.

I could visualize her downcast look of disappointment. Things got very quiet.

Now, I want you to understand, I'm not the type who easily hands money out my car window to the guy standing on the corner with his illegibly written cardboard sign.

However, if you heard the stories of the people I have helped: like hair-cuts, food, or clothing, you might question *why*. It's been a while since I've felt God whisper in my spirit, "Will you bless this one?"

As I stood there in the changing room, I sensed His still small familiar voice, *Bless her.* An excitement rose within me. I grabbed my purse but couldn't remember how much cash I had on hand. I seldom carry it because I use plastic.

When I checked, I found only 5 one-dollar bills. I was so disappointed I didn't have more. Nonetheless, I decided it was better than not giving anything at all.

Before I knew it, I went into an adrenalin mode, gathering my things together and walking out of my changing room. My heart was racing because I wanted to remain anonymous.

Now visualize this: the doors to the changing rooms were about 7' high with a space above them but no space below. I am 5'6". I had the dollar bills in my hand, and stood on my tip toes, to throw them over the top of the door.

I heard the young mother say, "Oh my goodness! Oh my goodness! There is money falling down!" By her reaction, you'd think they were twenties instead of five measly ones. She sounded shocked and hopefully it didn't scare the children; but they remained absolutely silent. The toddler must have known what money looked like and what it could buy.

I ducked down and wound my way through the clothing racks as I hurried on my way to the check-out station. She didn't see me and if anyone else did, they probably thought I was shop-lifting and headed for the exit.

My heart was racing and my hands were shaking as I reached the counter. I thought, *how silly, why am I responding this way?* Suddenly, I was brought back to reality when I heard the cashier say, "Ma'am, may I help you?"

Thankfully, I had my credit card to make the purchase. I looked at the cashier and said, "Sir, please listen carefully, I am going to give you a message for someone. If a young mother comes here with a baby and her toddler, to purchase an inexpensive top, and if she says, 'The weirdest thing happened to me in the changing room; someone threw some money over the door to my dressing room.' Please give her a message for me...will you?" I could tell he was uncertain as to what he was agreeing to. Hesitantly he answered with a slow, "Shuurre." So, I continued, "Also, tell her the lady who did it, wants me to tell you that God really loves you!" Then I added, "Sir, have you got the message?"

The young man's mouth dropped and with a glazed look of, *Lady, are you for real?,* he moved his head in a very *slow yes* response, as he looked me directly in the eye.

I felt sorry for the poor guy but I walked out of the store with the satisfaction that the young mother had been blessed, in such a simple way. She didn't need to know who the weird lady was who had rained the dollar bills upon her.

> *I'm amazed how a simple experience of*
> *giving can fill one's heart with such joy.*

Later, I got to thinking how sometimes the people who need to be blessed the most are the ones closest to us. Our spouse, a lonely parent, a rebellious child, a frowning grocery store clerk, an ornery boss, a fellow employee, etc.

If you are really open to be a blessing, without any expectations in return, the opportunities are endless. It doesn't necessarily take money; it may be simply a smile, a listening ear, or a kind word.

Try doing an experiment daily: Ask God to show you if there is a person *He* wants you to bless, as you go through your day.

Now, go be a blessing and "PAY IT FORWARD."

PRODUCER of STARWARS

Prayer is always the answer to any
concern or lost opportunity.

When this experience took place, we were in Ashland, Oregon, visiting family over the 4th of July holiday. I had been preparing dinner and needed to rush to the grocery store to pick up a couple items.

As I entered the store, I noticed a tall, slender, and gorgeous woman in her 60s. She was stunning and carried herself like a model. She also dressed like she was wealthy and wore classic-style clothing.

I thought, *it sure would be interesting to know her story.* But I wasn't about to ask questions. I was in a hurry, so I rushed to pick up my two items.

When I reached the check-out stand, two people were already in line.

Within seconds, a voice behind me said, "Can you believe how unusual these roses are?" When I turned around, that same attractive lady was standing behind me, holding a dozen lime-green-colored roses.

They truly were unusual, so I responded, "Those *are* beautiful! I don't think I've ever seen that color of rose." I smiled at her, then turned back to face the cashier.

That same lady then asked if I was from Ashland. I wanted to be gracious, so I turned around again and told her where our home was located and how we happened to be visiting my husband's parents.

I knew she was not interested in me. Most Divine Appointments have an agenda, a need to talk about his or her personal life.

As expected, she continued with her story. "My husband and I moved to Southern Oregon from California because he's dying of an incurable disease." My heart stirred with deep compassion after she shared her sad news.

Hardly having a moment to take a breath, she continued. "My husband was the original producer of the early Star Wars movies."

I thought, *"What? No wonder she looks like she just stepped out of the finest clothing stores in Hollywood. I'm sure her husband made a sizeable income!"*

My thoughts continued: *Doesn't she realize she is sharing personal information and I don't even know her name?* And I didn't ask because I had no plans to make further conversation until, out of nowhere, she added "I've been searching into different spiritual directions," (At this point, I had no idea this was my Divine Appointment.)

Now she *really* had my attention! I had no clue where this conversation was going, but without any thought, I responded to her "spiritual directions" comment by gently saying, "Really? I'm so grateful I've found the spiritual answer for *my* life."

I hoped I didn't sound prideful. However, after I heard my words, I thought, *that's not how I wanted to respond. If I never have another opportunity to see her, I would want to say something that would point her to Jesus.*

I knew beyond a shadow of a doubt that *Jesus was the one for whom she was searching.*

Sadly, I couldn't get into deep conversation because my family was waiting for me. I felt so torn. I thought, w**hat can I do Lord, what can I say**?

Suddenly, I was interrupted by the cashier who was waiting for me to pay for my groceries. After I paid, I realized this stately looking lady was clearly *not* about to let me go. (It's interesting how even when we have personal distractions that might prevent us from God's plan, He will work overtime to attempt to make His assignments possible!)

As I turned to leave, she said, "I need to talk more with you, can we exchange phone numbers?" I didn't have a cell phone that year, so I suggested my e-mail address.

Candidly, as I wrote it down, I never expected to hear from her again. This is often the pattern with strangers who approach me.

However, I was delighted to see her in my e-mail Inbox the next morning!

You might be thinking, w*hy would you even want to communicate with a complete stranger?* My response would be, w*hy wouldn't I?* I knew she was searching for truth. If God could use me to share His truth, I would be honored to do so.

I so wish I could say this story didn't end here, but, after my last email contact, making arrangements to meet, I never received another email from her.

I was deeply disappointed.

As I look back, I so desperately wish I had been better prepared to speak a word of encouragement and hope, instead of focusing solely on my dinner preparations.

It has been over a decade since this experience took place. In the end, I felt I had missed a great opportunity to share the hope for which this lady was searching.

However, in my disappointment, I've learned to accept that no matter how these stories end, I cannot give up hope. I will trust God to complete the story and will glean what He wants me to learn from each encounter.

The Bible tells to always be prepared to give an answer to anyone who asks us to give the reason for our hope (1 Peter 3:15b). I simply was distracted and unprepared.

Actually, the main reason I'm even sharing this short unfinished story is to also convey what I learned from this situation, in preparation for any future Divine Appointments.

If only I had taken the time to share a short word that would have given her a hunger to learn the truth in all her searching. I could have said something like:

> *God has created an emptiness in all our hearts that only He can fill. We can spend years searching into every religion and never find peace because Jesus is the truth for which you are searching. God loves you and He wants to fill you with hope for your future. May I encourage you to find a Bible and read the Book of John? You will discover how God provided His son, JESUS, who died on the cross for our sins. It's not about following a bunch of rules. We can never be good enough to reach a perfect God. However, God did not leave us stranded. He wants us to experience His love, joy and peace on this earth, and to be secure in knowing where we will spend eternity when we die.*

Over the years of unusual encounters that God has brought into my life, I finally learned the importance to be more spiritually prepared. The most important preparation is to start my day the night before and to get to bed early.

Then, the next morning, to rise early to meet with Jesus, not coffee, checking Facebook, or checking messages on my iPhone. He desires to be *first* in my day. He actually longs to have an intimate relationship with us.

Having an early quiet time without interruption is so precious! (For those who have to have your coffee, I'm sure God understands).

I ask the Lord to awaken me during the early morning hours. I want to be prepared, no matter who He puts in my path. I know He will be faithful to give me His words of hope, and will draw others to Himself.

My life verse says it all:

> *"The Lord God has given me His words of wisdom, so that I know how to comfort those in need. Morning by morning He awakens me and opens my understanding to His will."* (Isaiah 50:4)

Life is so full of joy when we allow Him to direct our day.

In this story, I was amazed I actually talked to the wife of one of the original producers of Star Wars. I so wish I could have shared Jesus with her, but when that didn't happen, I began to fervently pray for her and her husband (which might have been what God intended anyway).

I have faith to believe that God answered my prayer. I have no doubt God brought someone into her life to share the truth and she invited Jesus into her heart and life.

PRAYER is always the answer to
any concern or lost opportunity.

I truly believe God finished what I had wanted to share because He is a faithful God!

Meeting a lady from southern California and I hail from Washington State, is not a coincidence. *God set it up!* He always does when I least expect it.

Some people call these experiences a "God-Wink"! I call each one a Divine Appointment, orchestrated by my precious Lord.

HOTEL BELLMAN

*A simple message, planted in the heart of a
stranger, can change the trajectory of his life.*

My husband's employer had scheduled us for a five
day stay at the exquisite Davenport Hotel, which
is well-known throughout the world. Craig was
there on a work-related assignment to meet with attorneys
for a deposition. Since we had previously lived in Spokane,
Washington, it was fun to return and keep myself
entertained while he was busy with work.

For those who have never had an occasion to stay at the
Davenport, it is a wonderful experience. It was reopened
after tens of millions of dollars were spent on the
renovation of this 100-year-old luxury hotel. We were
always so grateful we could stay free!

On our last morning at the Davenport, my husband left for
appointments and I hurried to get packed and ready for our
return trip home. The plan was to pick him up at the office,
after he called.

Ten minutes before I planned to leave, I hit the
Valet/Bellman button on the hotel phone and after one
ring, I heard, "Mrs. Korthase," with a cheerful and low

masculine voice, "Would you like your car brought up?" He obviously knew that Room 314 was checking out and I would need my car, but what really amazed me was that he pronounced my name correctly. That seldom happens. There was just something special I sensed as I talked with him those few short moments.

I took the elevator down and walked to the outside booth for the valet service. The air was quite crisp that fall morning. Three bellmen were standing at the large entry doors as I asked, "Are any of you the gentleman who answered Room 314 when I called for my car?" They each responded, "No," at the same time and then one of them said, "It must have been Andrew."

I was told Andrew was at the property across the street and would return in a half-hour. As I started to get in my car, I received a call from my husband. He informed me that he needed another half-hour to finish up a few more details before he could leave. At that moment, I had no idea the Lord had planned this delay for a purpose.

I was delighted to have a few more minutes and decided to go back into the lobby, sit by the fireplace, and just enjoy the ambiance of this elegant hotel.

As I turned around to head for the lobby, I heard one of the bellmen say, "Mrs. Korthase, here is Andrew right now." He pointed at a new white Mercedes that had just entered the round-a-bout in the covered area where I was standing. The young man was sitting in the driver's seat and I walked over to the car he had just delivered.

I said, "Are you Andrew?" He said, "Yes." As he reached out to shake my hand, he asked, "How can I help you?"

Wow, I thought, *He certainly has a firm hand shake and knows the importance of looking his customer in the eye.*

Then I said, "Andrew, I just want to say how impressed I was when you answered room 314 this morning. Your deep voice sounded warm and gracious, but most of all, you genuinely sounded like you cared about your customer." He shook my hand again and then thanked me for the encouraging words.

I like giving *good reports* to employees and their manager because I'm sure they get plenty of negative reports.

As I walked over to my car, I realized he was following me. The conversation began as he asked me if I was heading home, and if I had enjoyed my stay at the Davenport. I responded with, "Staying at the Davenport is always wonderful!"

I asked if he was the manager of his department and he said, "Yes, I'm the supervisor." The conversation continued, and all I did was stand and listen, looking interested in what he was saying. I heard highlights of Andrew's life:

He had worked at the hotel for eight years. He & his girlfriend had split up two weeks earlier. His father suddenly died six years before His mother and younger brother moved to be near him. He was 30 years old and finishing his degree. He had taken four years off from college after his father's death. He had struggled with his father's passing and had gone through stages of anger, bitterness, and eventually went through a lot of counseling and…He was still searching!

I listened to him talk for about 20 minutes. The whole time, I thought, *God, why is he sharing all this personal information with me? Do you have something you want me to share with him?*

I didn't want to be too direct, because I might scare him, so I said, "Andrew, you've experienced a lot of pain in the past few years. You know, as you were talking, I was wondering if you've had any religious training in your earlier years?" His response was, "Yes, my parents were church-goers, but my family has really been disillusioned with the church."

I responded, "You know, there are some good churches, but in my own experience I've learned that the answer is having a personal relationship with God's son, Jesus

Christ." He appeared interested in what I was sharing, so I continued.

"Matter-of-fact, my husband was diagnosed with a very rare cancer two years ago; it turned out to be a very uncertain time and difficult experience to walk through. We would never have survived that painful experience without the Lord. He gave us hope, and carried us through each difficult and painful step of that experience."

As I was talking, I was also praying *in my spirit* that the Lord would show me *what* to say next. I knew I only had moments before I had to leave.

Suddenly, unplanned words came out of my mouth, "Andrew, do you have a Bible?" He looked at me with surprise, saying, "You know what? I just found my old Bible a few days ago!"

I continued, "Andrew, I'd like to encourage you to begin reading the Book of John, in the New Testament." Immediately, he responded, "John? That's my Dad's name!"

"You know Andrew," I continued, "I believe God has a real purpose for you and He longs to have a personal relationship with you. So, as you open your Bible to start reading in the Book of John, just talk to God and say, 'God, I really don't know you, except what my parents have told me and what I learned in church, but I want to get to know you better. Please show me that You are real and speak to my heart. Help me to understand what I'm reading.'"

By this time, I thought I would have lost his interest in continuing the conversation or he would at least show some concern that the other employees might be wondering why he was standing there talking to an older woman for so long.

Instead, he said, "Wow, I *will* start reading! Thank you for your words of encouragement. I'd really like to learn more." He sounded hungry to find something that would fill the emptiness he obviously had been trying to fill.

Before I left, he grabbed a small piece of paper and wrote down his name and e-mail address. I told him I would write and see how things were going. He said, "I'd really appreciate it."

However, like so many other Divine Appointments, when I meet a stranger, they are enthusiastic to share the raw and painful areas of their life. Then, after time passes, I can only imagine them feeling embarrassed that they talked with a complete stranger about such personal issues.

I emailed Andrew, but I never received a response from him. I was deeply disappointed.

But I'm convinced that someday, when I'm in heaven, Andrew will walk up to me and say, "I'm the bellman you shared Jesus with at the Davenport Hotel. And, that night, I started reading the Book of John in my old Bible. As I read, Jesus began to speak to my heart. In time, I asked Him into my heart and life and, *wow*, my life changed forever! And guess what, I found a good church and met my beautiful Christian wife. My mom and brother came to know Jesus too. Thank you for taking the time to introduce me to my Savior."

I am not imagining these thoughts. I truly believe this is what God did and someday I will see him again.

We never know how a simple word, planted in the heart of a stranger, can change an ordinary life into one that produces abundant eternal fruit.

IN THE PIT

*God has given us the opportunity
to choose Him or to resist Him.*

Years ago, when my husband was transferred to a new city, I ended up in daily contact with several neighborhood latchkey children. It didn't take long before I also had an opportunity to meet one of the mothers of the young brothers in this motley group.

From the very beginning of my friendship with Adair, I could see that her family desperately needed Jesus.

The father, Mike, was a fireman and filled all the boxes of how firemen often live, when they have a lifestyle of putting themselves first. Adair was obviously feeling insecure and sensed something was wrong in her marriage. Of course, when she asked him if he was having an affair, he would lie and put her down for asking such a silly question.

Over time, she began seeing symptoms that scared her. She'd tell me, "I think my husband is falling apart, and I don't know what's wrong. She felt like she was doing everything to meet his every need but *nothing* she did seemed to help. He was showing signs of a nervous breakdown.

She and I often met and talked, and in time, she wanted to know more about Jesus. She saw her need to make Him part of her life. With her troubled marriage, she now had the Lord to walk with her through everything she was facing.

One late evening, as I was praying, I had a vision about Mike. It was so intense I knew I needed to share it with him, but I wanted it to be in God's timing. Then, when He finally gave me peace, I decided to write a letter. This is what I shared:

Dear Mike,

You may be surprised to receive a letter from me but I feel I need to share something really important with you. Each time I have started to write, I've hesitated because I've thought, "He'll think I'm crazy, or, it's none of her business." But, I hope you understand that God has given us a real love for your family. We care about what you do with your life and how it affects your family. So, please be open to what I have to say.

In the Pit

Some weeks ago, I had a very unusual experience, that relates to you. Previously, I had been spending a lot of time praying for your family because I could see the turmoil you all were experiencing. As I prayed I suddenly saw a vision of a large deep pit in the cold ground. The pit was full of quicksand. You were in the pit, but every time you tried to get out, you slipped just a little bit deeper. Around the pit's edge were long ropes that you were trying to grab, one at a time. Each rope represented different things: material possessions, money or other women. When you grabbed a rope to pull yourself out, it would break and you fell back into the quicksand of despair.

However, at the edge of this pit, there was also a man reaching out to you with his strong hand, offering to pull you out; when you saw that He was Jesus, you were not interested. You were determined to do it your own way! You knew that taking His hand would mean letting go of your pride in controlling your own life. So, you kept resisting the hand that could pull you out of the desperate situation where your very life was being threatened.

Mike, without allowing Jesus to change our lives, we are all in the same miserable pit. Life has no meaning or peace; we go through life, only existing. And, on the inside, we feel like we're being crushed by the quicksand around us. You see, God has given us the opportunity to choose Him or to resist Him. He could have made us as puppets, where we have no choice; instead, He created us with a God-shaped-vacuum in our lives and until we invite Him into our heart – asking His forgiveness of our sins and asking Him to fill that emptiness, we will keep running, keep searching and keep trying to find something or someone to fill that void, while we continue to sink deeper into the quicksand.

Go ahead and think, 'I knew she would start preaching to me.' Well Mike, if I knew you had cancer and I also knew the cure, would I sit back and let you die, saying nothing? NO! This is no different because you are dying within, emotionally and spiritually.

I hope you are understanding what I'm sharing. Believe me, religion is not the answer, with a list of do's and don'ts. The real answer is Jesus!

He's the one who took our punishment and died in our place for all our sins (wrong choices).

I'm enclosing a small booklet that explains more clearly what I have shared. You can throw it away or save it and read one day when you've tried everything else and you come to the end of yourself. Jesus will still be there waiting for you; still holding out His hand to pull you out of the pit; still knocking at your heart's door and waiting for you to invite Him into your heart and life.

Please understand that I am not going to bring this topic up again, unless you do. When I see you, I'll say nothing nor will I put pressure on you, but we will continue to pray.

We love you Mike and we believe that God has a purpose for your life.

Karen

He never responded. I assumed he destroyed the letter. I knew I had to leave it with God.

Then, one day, before Mike's divorce to Adair, she found the letter under some clothes in one of his drawers. She told me that it was unusual that he would have kept it. We were both certain that God had spoken to his heart but he wasn't ready to take God's Hand to get out of the Pit.

I pray that it will happen before he passes from this earth into eternity. And, I pray that every time he sees that letter, God's spirit will speak to his heart and draw him to Himself.

PALE PINK DRESS

This experience gave me more of a
longing to eternally be with Jesus.

Our home in Eastern Washington was for sale and I was in the process of packing several personal items, in preparation for our movers to arrive. My husband had been transferred back to Seattle, to begin his new job. He was waiting for the day I would join him.

One morning, during my packing, my niece called.

I could tell by her voice that something was terribly wrong! I braced myself to hear the difficult news.

Their first grandchild, baby Hannah, had been born full-term, but had major complications during the delivery. She went on to explain how the baby had been placed on life-support. I gasped as I learned the heart-breaking news and fought back the tears.

"Oh Karen, please pray for a miracle!" she cried. My heart ached for their pain and I couldn't imagine how their son and daughter-in-law were dealing with the uncertainty of their precious baby's life.

There was nothing I could say to bring comfort, but I knew I could pray.

I was grateful our entire family believed in prayer and knew God was a miracle-working God. For three days, we all "stormed" the gates of heaven. Our faith was strong, and we totally expected a miracle.

On the third night after her call, I went to bed, turned off the lights, and began praying for baby Hannah as I had the other two nights.

I was told she was an absolutely angelic-looking baby. From the moment she was taken into Children's hospital, the nurses and doctors became very attached to her, and she was loved by everyone who cared for her.

> *I was certain her precious little spirit heard constant words of love and felt prayers going up for her all over the world. I was confident that every moment, she was being cradled in the arms of Jesus.*

Later that evening, the doctors knew they needed to have 'the talk' with her parents. They tried to be as gentle as possible, carefully choosing their words, but no parent is ever prepared for that kind of heart-wrenching conversation.

Soon, the doctor entered the room and facing the parents, he said, "Because we're not seeing any changes taking place in Hannah. we believe we've come to a place where a decision needs to be made."

The family understood what the doctor meant by the word *decision*. However, the thought of removing her life-support was a pain that no parent should ever have to experience. They knew they *couldn't* give up hope. After all, they were still waiting for a miracle!

When I went to bed that night, I, too, prayed for a miracle. I cried out to God with all of my heart. Suddenly, my prayer was interrupted by a...*VISION*.

I was standing on a large field of short, fresh-cut, thick, green grass. Everything surrounding this scene was blank, with an early evening light high-lighting four individuals: three adults standing several yards in front of me, and a 2-year-old barefoot toddler standing in the middle. She wore a delicate *pale pink dress* that was especially beautiful.

I was invisible to them but I could clearly see every movement and expression on their faces. The child in the center, who was standing tall, held both arms out-stretched to her left and right sides; the palms of her hands were facing up, as though she was waiting to receive something. Her head, covered with soft blonde curls was turned to the right, where she was focused on her parents' faces, several yards away. They, too, were standing with their arms out-stretched towards her.

No words were spoken. Longingly, they looked at their precious child. She knew *they* were waiting and hoping she would run to them. They knew *she* was waiting for them to let her go. She was aware that she couldn't face the man to her left, until she was released by her parents.

As she studied their every move, waiting, she suddenly saw her mommy and daddy gently bow their heads towards her, signaling…they were letting go.

As she turned to glance at the person to her left, she clearly knew who He was! He was kneeling on one knee, majestically dressed in a pure white linen robe, with His arms out-stretched towards her, the same distance away as her parents were, to her right.

IT WAS JESUS!

Oh, the joy of being in His Presence!

In slow motion, she turned to run to Him, and as she ran, she sang out her words with the sweetest heavenly sound, "Thank you, mommy… thank you, daddy… I love you!" She ran into the arms of Jesus and He gently held her, softly speaking in her ear, *"I'm so glad you've come home!"*

As quickly as the vision began…IT ENDED!

I opened my eyes to the dark room and quickly turned on the lamp next to my bed. "NOOO!" I loudly whispered. "It can't end!" Immediately, I turned the light off, laid back down and closed my eyes, praying, "Please Jesus, let me go back and see more of the vision!"

Sadly, it didn't happen.

As I opened my eyes again, I realized how precious the vision had been and what I had personally experienced. The amazing JOY couldn't be compared to the joy we think we experience on this earth. *It was so pure.* It was like nothing I had ever experienced.

Tears welled up in my eyes. I realized I was ruined forever because it gave me a longing to see Jesus and to be with Him in heaven. There really were no words to clearly explain how I felt.

After the vision ended, I rushed to the computer to type out the story. I wanted to hang on to every thought and not forget any part of it. I knew that getting it in print would help me remember the details that I never wanted to lose.

During this time, I made a call to my husband Craig. He was in Seattle and I was thrilled to learn he was at the hospital, waiting for the parents and grand-parents to return to the NICU (Neonatal Intensive Care Unit). They had found a quiet place to be alone to pray.

Craig and their pastor were in the waiting room, when he answered my call. After I shared my vision with my husband, he passed the story on to the family, after they returned.

As they entered the NICU ward, to their delight, while they were gone, the nurses, without being asked, had removed Hannah's baby hospital gown. They dressed her in a sweet little *pale pink dress!* It was like the dress in the vision!

Before the painful decision was made, the parents & grandparents were allowed more time with Hannah. As they lovingly held her close, they whispered their love to her and thanked the Lord for the short time they had with her. Then…it was time to let her go, but they still held on to hope for a miracle.

They released her into the arms of Jesus; He could either heal her on this earth, or take her home to be with Him in heaven.

It wasn't until they heard the vision story again, they realized how miraculous it was that the nurses had dressed Hannah in the same pale pink colored dress as in the vision.

Eighteen years later, God gave me another short vision one night.

Hannah was in Heaven and she looked so joyful! I saw her skipping with Jesus, as she held on to His hand. Once again, she was wearing a pale pink dress and looked to be about 5 years of age. She was as beautiful and precious as she was when she left this earth.

As I've reflected on these amazing experiences, I felt deeply humbled. I asked God, "Why did you trust me to experience those two precious visions of Hannah?" I knew I could only trust that He had a purpose in it. Through tears, I thanked Him for allowing me to be His messenger, and have the opportunity to share her story with others.

Someday, I will get to meet Hannah, when I, too, step into eternity with Jesus.

SEAT 7-C

I was anxious to see what God had in mind for 7-C.

was in Palm Springs preparing for renters to arrive at our condo. I *wasn't* eager to return to rainy Seattle, but I had a speaking engagement and needed to make final preparations.

The night before my departure, I prayed that the Lord would open a seat on an earlier flight. In my spirit I heard 7-C. I had *no* clue what that was all about. I knew I had been assigned a seat towards the back because no front row or aisle seats were available. Frustration!

The next morning, I awakened early and began to pray about my flight.

I said, "Lord, forgive me for being frustrated. I choose to trust You to put me on the flight that You want me to be on." Once again, I asked, "Lord, should I try to get an earlier flight so I can get home sooner?"

I heard 7-C again in my spirit and began to think it was a figment of my imagination. I even asked the Lord if that could be a possibility. Again, I heard, 7-C. Now, I thought things were really getting weird, but I said, "OK Lord, if this is you speaking in my spirit, I will listen and obey and stick with my original plans. If it is all my imagination, I'll just hope that You have a purpose in it."

My neighbors, Joe and Lucy, welcomed me to their condo after my renters arrived. I would have one night with them before leaving the next day on my flight. I thought, *OK God, I think I understand that this is all part of Your plan.* I knew they were looking forward to my visit. Then, once again, I heard 7-C. I was getting used to that number and didn't give it any more thought.

The next morning, I called the airlines one last time to see if there were any last-minute changes for seating. The reservations lady said, "I'm sorry, there are no seats toward the front. I wish I could have…" She stopped speaking and then said, "Wait a minute, seat 7-C has just opened up!" I answered, "What?! Are you sure?" "Absolutely," she answered!

Was God laughing? I knew He had to be thinking, *"Haven't I been telling you all along that I was saving that seat for you?"* I was so grateful!

The reservations lady couldn't understand my excitement and appreciation. It wasn't about moving to a new seat. At this point, I was excited to see what God had in mind for seat 7-C.

Before I left, I weighed my suitcase. *Oh no*, I thought. *I have more I still need to add*! Joe kept picking it up and saying, "Karen, you have way over 50 pounds now and it's going to cost you big money!"

Fear began to grip my heart because I only had $20 on me and I felt God wanted me to give it to a lady who worked at Budget Rent-a-Car. I had met and talked with her days earlier and knew she had major health problems and was struggling financially.

On the way to the airport, I had prayed, "Lord, I know this fear is not of you so I ask you to remove it, and I ask you to either blind the eyes of the airline attendant or cause this suitcase not to weigh over 50 pounds."

When I reached the terminal, I walked over to the Alaska Airlines desk and lifted my very heavy suitcase up on the stainless scale. Lo and behold, it read 45pounds!

I thought, *that can't be possible.* In disbelief, I foolishly took it off the scale while the attendant was busy doing other things, and then re-placed it on the scale.

Once again it read 45 pounds! In my heart I thought, *Lord, you did that for me! Thank you.*

I still had the $20 in my pocket.

After checking in, I walked over to the Budget Rent-a-Car counter. I have had contacts with the employees many times and pray for them almost daily because they each have serious needs.

I stood in line, letting others go in front of me so I'd be sure to end up with the lady who had helped me days earlier. When it was my turn, I gave her the information regarding my rental and told her I was ready to check out. She pulled up the paperwork and I asked, "What's the final price?" I knew what it should have been, but when she handed me the paperwork, it was *$20 less* than I had expected!

In my thoughts I said, *Lord, you have such a sense of humor. Thank you once again.*

We continued to talk about her health issue, and before I left, we exchanged phone numbers and then I said, "By the way, "I'm supposed to give this to you." I handed her the $20 bill and a blank look came over her face. "I can't accept this," she answered. "Oh yes you can," I responded. And before I walked away, I touched her hand and said, "The Lord bless you."

I had not given any more thought to 7-C. I just went to the boarding area and waited. When it was time to board the plane, I prayed in my thoughts, *Lord, I would love to just have some quiet time to work on my speaking engagement, but if you have a Divine Appointment with someone next to me, I'm willing to be available.*

A nice lady and her very odd husband scooted in seats A and B. She was quite a talker. There was conversation all the way for almost 3 hours.

About 10 minutes before we landed, when things were finally silent, I turned to the 90+ year old woman across the aisle from me and said, "Ma'am, I would like to help you with your suitcase when we land." She tried to tell me she didn't need any help, but the young lady sitting next to her, in seat 7-F, piped up and said, "Yes, I will help you also."

We left the plane, helped the elderly lady, and passed her on to her daughter who was standing in the waiting area. She informed her mother that she had ordered a wheelchair. The older woman said, "Oh, that's not necessary. I can walk on my own." At that point, I gently leaned down to her eye level and said, "Honey, you might want to listen to your daughter because it's a very long distance from this terminal to the subway train, and then from the train to the main terminal." She smiled and the daughter expressed gratefulness for our assistance and encouragement to her mother.

The lady who sat in seat 7-F who also assisted the elderly woman, walked with me as we rushed to catch the subway to the main terminal. As we entered the train, while huffing and puffing, she exclaimed, "These crazy hot flashes! I'm sick of them. I've tried everything and nothing works!"

At this point I had no plans, nor even a desire to get involved in sharing about the product I knew could help her. I just wanted to get to my destination. Without any thought, I found myself saying, "I know, I used to deal with them also." She responded, "What did you do?" I proceeded to say, "Well, first of all, you are too young to be having hot-flashes. You must only be in your 30's." She laughed and informed me she was actually 50 years old. It was hard to believe. Then, once again, she said, "So, what did you do?"

Oh no, I thought, *I don't want to get into this explanation*, but she was standing there in suspense as though I had the perfect answer for her dilemma. I began trying to be as short in my responses as I possibly could.

I continued, "Actually, I was taking a product hoping the Chronic Fatigue Syndrome and Fibromyalgia would …." She grabbed my arm and said, "Did you say Fibromyalgia? I can't believe I'm hearing you say this!"

I began to think she was upset with my conversation because she became so emotional. Then she explained. "I have been dealing with Fibromyalgia for years and am on strong medication because I can't deal with the pain. How is it possible that you are here to share this information with me?"

It was time to get off the train and rush to the baggage claim area. It was getting late and I knew my husband was waiting in the cell phone lot. Besides, we had another hour of driving time before arriving home. We would be rising at 4am the next morning and I was in no mood to talk. Why should I? I had missed my seat 7-C appointment that God had planned for me. I *wasn't* excited to talk to this lady about her health anyway, until the Lord softly whispered in my spirit, *"This is your appointment."*

Now, why in the world would God want me to talk to *this* gal about her health? What kind of a Divine Appointment could that be? And, why would I even question God since I've had so many similar experiences?

It was impossible to talk while we were in the crowd of people. Everyone was rushing to the baggage claim area and believe it or not, everyone found their luggage except this lady and me. What were the chances?

My luggage had a lime green & white strap, so that I could identify it easily. I didn't see it *anywhere*. After the conveyor belt had been mostly emptied, only three suitcases remained, going around and around…one black and two turquoise suitcases.

Within moments, the other gal came rushing to me and said, "These two cases look identical to mine, but they aren't mine. The person who owns them must have taken mine by mistake."

By this time, I decided to take a better look at the one remaining black suitcase. Sure enough, it belonged to me.

Oh my, someone had decided they liked my colorful lime green strap.

I grabbed my bag and started to leave. I *still* wasn't convinced that the young woman was my Divine Appointment. I'm a slow learner.

"Wait," I heard her say, "Can I get your phone number? I want to talk with you further about the product you are taking. By the way, my name is Barbara."

I gave her my name and then I looked into her eyes and said, "Actually, I need to tell you something. My seat assignment was originally in the back of the plane, and when I called the airlines to change it, 7-C opened up at the last minute."

She said, "Actually, I had also been placed in the back and was reassigned to 7-F."

I continued, "But there's more. I had considered trying to take an earlier flight. However, I strongly felt God was preparing me to have an important conversation with someone. I wondered if that person could be you?"

She didn't act surprised whatsoever, and responded like she agreed with what I was saying. I had only met this woman minutes before, but she hugged me good-bye and asked me to make sure I called her.

The next day, I hesitantly made the call. Surprisingly, we also made plans to meet for lunch.

Sadly, that evening, her husband informed her that they were going on a week's vacation to their new condo in Eastern Washington. She called to let me know the change of plans and added, "I still want to meet with you when I return, and I **will** call you!"

I felt certain this Divine Appointment would take place because God had orchestrated it all, starting with the 7-C impression He had given me many times before I even boarded the plane.

However, she never called. When I tried to reach her by phone there was never an answer.

I was deeply disappointed because I was looking forward to sharing the *Good News* with her; not about the product I had been taking, but instead, information of HOPE that could change her life forever.

UPDATE: This experience took place in 2008. Each time I reread this story in my Word files, I had wished I could talk to her again. However, after all these years, I had no phone number, e-mail or home address.

Then, in 2020, God brought her to mind several times. So, I prayed in my thoughts, *God, I have no way of contacting Barbara, but if you have a reason why you would like us to meet again, I ask for your miracle working power to do the impossible and help me to find Barbara.*

Well, recently I miraculously found a box of old papers, and as I was tossing several of them, I found a paper with Barb's name and contact information!

The date on it reminded me that we had met on Alaska Airlines, seat 7-C and 7-F. I felt like doing cartwheels because of my excitement. God had answered my simple prayer!

So, I called the first number, but it was disconnected. Thankfully, there was a second number which I quickly dialed and was able to leave a message.

Barbara immediately returned my call. I was glad to get reconnected. And though her response was less than enthusiastic, which was totally different than what I expected would happen, I knew I couldn't question why. So, I gave her my cell number and trust that someday God will prompt her to call me.

I still believe God had a purpose for our meeting. And, I will continue to pray for His *perfect will* to be completed.

CLASS REUNION

Was I willing to be obedient to
what God had called me to do?

M y 10th year High School Class Reunion was only weeks away. I was being a typical woman, thinking about what I would wear. I wanted to look my best. However, I had no idea what God would ask of me concerning this reunion.

I was raring to attend this event, but I knew I would be alone. My first husband's death in the Vietnam war, three years prior, had given me a more serious perspective on life. I had walked with the Lord for many years, and this loss anchored a deeper faith in my spirit.

As a young widow trying to navigate through life, that experience opened several opportunities to share my faith in speaking to groups throughout my home state of Washington.

God had filled my heart with hope for my future and gave me a message for those who had lost hope through the deep trials in their own lives.

Days before I attended the gathering, I sensed God's gentle whisper asking me to be available to share a short message with my classmates. I was certain I had misunderstood His voice because the planning committee had already made their preparations for the program.

As time got closer to the reunion date, I heard His tender whisper in my spirit again, saying, *share at the reunion*. Speaking didn't scare me, but the more I thought about it, the more unsettled I felt about *who* my audience would be.

When that evening finally arrived, I walked into the crowded room filled with couples and felt a bit uneasy at first. However, in a short time, I connected with several old friends. It appeared that many were looking happy, successful and full of life. Yet, I wondered if some of them were truly *that* put-together?

I heard His familiar whisper in my spirit for the third time, but dismissed it again. Over the weeks, I had sensed what God wanted me to share and I was prepared. However, I felt a *fight* inside my spirit hearing all the reasons why it wouldn't be possible.

I had noticed the tables were set in a banquet-style arrangement. In my thoughts, I wrestled with God and thought how impossible it looked for me to share my heart in this venue. The room appeared too crowded to allow ease of walking up to the stage.

After several minutes of mingling with my old friends, I heard the master of ceremony say on the microphone,

"We're ready to begin now. Please come and take your seats."

Somehow, I ended up sitting near the center of all the tables and realized I was crammed in and wouldn't be able to get out without making a big scene. The tables, as I had observed earlier, were positioned too close together.

The program began and the time passed quickly with lots of laughter and fun memories being shared. Then, I heard the MC say, "This has been a great evening. But, before we close, I wonder if there is anyone who has anything they would like to say?"

Suddenly, my throat got dry and my heart began to race. I knew it was my cue to stand up, but I felt frozen in place. I thought, *what's wrong with me? Speaking in front of others has never bothered me before.*

The MC had waited and looked over the large group of people and saw that no one had responded to his question. I wanted to obey what God had asked of me but it just looked too impossible to get out of my row and disturb all those behind me. Actually, I began to think …

> *God wouldn't want me to make a fool of myself*
> *in front of all my classmates, would He?*

I continued to rationalize, but decided I'd better pray. In my heart I said, "Lord Jesus, I really want to be certain that *You* did ask me to share with my classmates. If You did, then have the MC ask that same question again and I will follow through."

I was certain it was too late and he would say, *if no one has anything to say, then we will be dismissed.* But NO! I heard the MC repeat, "Is there anyone who has anything they would like to say?" I was frozen in place.

I so desperately wanted to obey God, but I felt weak and shaky and all I could do was continue to question Him…**All because I had allowed myself to struggle far too long**. If only I had listened and obeyed His voice in the beginning. It wouldn't have given an opportunity to play games with my doubting mind.

The program ended. The feeling of FAILURE wrapped around me like a cocoon. The tightness on my chest caused me to want to run away. I had to get out of there, to get alone and cry. My heart felt like Peter in the Bible when he denied Jesus three times. I felt like I, too, had denied my precious Lord.

Could He ever redeem the loss I had created
by my NOT responding to His will?

I felt my actions had grieved my Lord. Thankfully, He assured me of His love and forgiveness. But, forgiving myself was much more difficult.

Over the years, each reunion was a reminder of what had happened all those many years before.

Then, 30 years after that 10th reunion, I once again heard His still small voice. He said, "Write a letter."

Over the years, I had drawn much closer to Him and was not as intimidated by what others thought. So, I began to pray, asking Him to clearly show me what He would have me write in a letter.

While struggling to write, I was reminded how saddened we all felt at each reunion, when the names of the students who had passed-on were read. I felt it was important to convey that it's not about a religion, but instead, the importance of a personal relationship with Jesus. They needed to be certain where they would spend eternity when taken from this earth.

As I wrote, I felt a compassionate boldness come over me.

I edited my letter over and over because I questioned my ability to express important truths. Yet, the most important thing was to be obedient to what God had called me to do.

After it was written, I contacted the reunion planning committee. I was told I would need to submit the letter to the committee to have it okayed. When the committee read it, some said it wouldn't be appropriate for it to be sent to everyone. However, I learned that one person stood up for me and said, "What harm could it do? Let her send it."

They allowed me to have all my classmates' addresses and gave permission for it to be sent. I began printing dozens of letters, handwriting all the addresses onto the envelopes, and licking all the stamps! Lastly, I prayed over them and mailed them.

It came time for the 40th reunion. As I entered the large room, I looked around and thought, *oh my goodness, everyone looks so old!* Thankfully, we were wearing name tags, because if the truth were told, I wasn't recognizable either.

My husband, Craig, was with me and we found a seat next to my best high school friend, Jane. I was hesitant about what others might say, regarding the letter they had each received. Several came up to me and gently said, "Thank you for your letter." Others said, "Boy you were brave; I could never have written a letter like that."

After we were all seated, dinner was served and later the program began. One of the guys from our class had been asked to speak that evening. Halfway through his talk, he abruptly stopped and turned to look directly at me! I thought, *oh no, what is he doing?* Then, he said, "I know we all received the same letter from one of our classmates. Although I don't agree with everything she shared, I respect her for what she did. She cared enough to write the letter and shared her personal concerns for each of us."

The entire time his eyes were on me, I had my head lowered. I *wasn't* embarrassed, instead, I was humbled.

When the program ended, several people apologized to me on behalf of our speaker. They expressed how he had embarrassed me. I thanked them for their kindness, but made certain they understood I had not been made uncomfortable. Instead, I was touched by his kindness and was deeply humbled. The letter shared why I had written it and how I had waited 30 years before I finally listened to what God had asked of me.

When we left the reunion, I told my husband that the Lord had **redeemed** what I had not done all those years before.

When we hesitate, He offers us His grace, mercy, and forgiveness to listen and follow His lead the next time. But, believe me…

It's worth listening and obeying the *first time* He whispers into our spirit!

A HIGHER PURPOSE

*You never know who will be spiritually
hungry and willing to hear about Jesus.*

Our son had invited me to fly back to Alexandria, Virginia to care for our two grandsons while he and my daughter-in-law attended a conference. I was thrilled to be asked.

My flight would be on United Airlines, with a stop-over in Denver, Colorado, and then on to Washington, D.C.

This had been a busy season with my husband in and out of the hospital for surgeries and chemo, during his cancer treatment.

I was tired and was looking forward to some quiet time on the airplane. Matter-of-fact, before I boarded, I even asked the Lord to give me a seat where I could have a peaceful, quiet time to rest...*without* any Divine Appointments.

However, as I boarded, I prayed in my thoughts, *Lord, you know best. If you have a divine appointment waiting for me, I'm willing and available.*

I walked down the aisle to seat 33D. I noticed a nice-looking young man seated by the window, with a pile of books, in the middle seat. It was a good indication he'd probably want to read, and he obviously didn't want to be disturbed. I didn't like the idea of being in the back of the plane, so I was thankful the middle seat was empty.

After I was settled in my seat, I sat back, closed my eyes and was delighted to have some quiet time to rest.

Within moments, I heard him shuffling through his books, choosing one to read. As I looked over at the book he had chosen, the extra-large letters on the edge of the book spelled out the word ABRAHAM.

I'm not certain how it started but I think I opened my mouth and words fell out. "That looks like an interesting book. Is it Abraham from the Old Testament in the Bible or someone else?"

I had no plans to enter into a conversation, but I felt like a willing puppet as words were being spoken through me. At this point, I hadn't realized that I was at the beginning of a Divine Appointment and God was giving me the words to say. It truly wasn't my plan.

My seat partner was John Solomon, a 30-year-old business man who had an amazing job where he traveled all over the world. He was engaged to a beautiful and talented young lady who was a daughter of someone who worked with the Billy Graham Organization. (I now wish I had written down all these details more clearly but that wasn't the purpose of this appointment).

Even with all his success, he knew there was still something missing in his life. He had been searching and looking at different religions. In our conversation, I learned he was half Jewish, and I got really excited because I love the Jewish people. Some years later, I learned that I, too, am part Jewish and was thrilled to learn this discovery. After all, the Bible calls them *His chosen people.*

As we were talking, the Lord showed me that I was to speak His truth and be gracious in sharing with him. I knew we didn't have much time because he would soon be getting off the plane in Denver.

After he shared how he had been searching, I gently said, "John, when God created us, He placed a God-shaped vacuum in our heart that can never be filled by anything apart from Him. We can search the entire world and study every religion, but the emptiness in our soul was created by God, and He is the only one who can fill it. You see, He gave His only son, Jesus, also a Jew, to fill that void in the heart of mankind. When Jesus died on the cross, He died for you and for me."

John was hanging on every word, so I continued. "Because of the sin in our lives, we could never reach a perfect God. But when Jesus shed His blood for us on the cross, and when we ask His forgiveness of our sins, we can be assured we will spend eternity with Him."

John had already realized that the Bible may have some answers because he had already started reading the Old Testament. (That's not where I would have started but because of his Jewish heritage, perhaps that's where God knew he needed to read. I normally encourage people, who are searching for the truth, to begin reading the Book of John, in the New Testament.).

I knew he was seriously interested when he pulled out his cell phone and started taking notes as we talked. He had shared that his dad was dying of cancer and he was going home to say goodbye.

I then asked if his father knew what would happen when he dies. He responded, "I'm really not sure." I continued, "Would you like to know some scriptures that you could read to your dad? These would help him understand the important choice he needs to make before he steps into eternity." John responded, "Yes, please."

This can be a difficult season for any of us when we face the upcoming loss of our parents. I was thankful when he received the scriptures with gratefulness.

I told John that if they didn't have a Bible, he could look them up on the Internet and print them out for his dad.

For all I know, the non-Christian son, may have ended up leading his Jewish father to a personal relationship with Jesus!

I wish I could have been there to witness what the Holy Spirit did with John and his dad. Believe me, I had several people praying with me and I'm certain the Holy Spirit had already been working in the father's heart before his son even arrived at their home.

Before we landed, I told him I was going to ask him the most important question he would ever be asked. I only had moments to communicate God's truth with him. I said, "John, if this plane went down before we landed, do you know where *you* would spend eternity?" He gave me the opportunity to share, in those few short moments, how he could know for certain. However, he told me he wanted more time to think through his decision.

After we landed, I got off the plane to walk around during the layover. We walked to the terminal and I was amazed that he hugged me goodbye and expressed that he felt God had orchestrated our time to talk on the flight.

I felt so blessed to have met this young man. As I talked with him, I felt God had a great plan for his future and I felt certain that he would soon make the most important decision of his life to become all that God created him to be. I'm praying and am anxious to hear from him some day.

I didn't get my needed nap that morning, after rising at 2a.m. to get to the airport. However, I felt so humbled by that precious experience with John. I sensed that God had planned the whole encounter. He placed us in those seats, gave me the thoughts to share (they certainly were not my own), and then when we went our separate ways, God filled me with amazing JOY, once again.

That trip was *not* just about visiting kids or loving on grandsons. God had…

A HIGHER PURPOSE.

FURNITURE STORE SALESMAN

The Lord can even use a simple shopping trip
to bring about a life-changing experience.

O ne afternoon, my husband and I decided to run to Costco for gas. In the process, we also decided to check out a new furniture store that was close by. Our living room furniture was looking a little old and worn.

As we walked up to the large entry of the store, I said, "These big stores always have a salesman waiting for the next person who walks in the door. I wish they would just let us leisurely walk around."

Before I knew it, the large door opened and a tall older gentleman greeted us. "Good afternoon, I'm Oscar."

We gave him our names and then he gave us a few directions and let us go and wander around, checking in with us only occasionally. Over the next hour, we looked over the entire store and were pleased with the sale prices, *plus* a 20% discount.

I couldn't get over the salesman. He was *so* patient. And, I noticed he kept tabs on us, but often paused to sit and rest on an arm of a sofa.

We weren't planning on buying anything but I did find a living room set I liked. We expressed our interest, so we all sat down to talk about the cost. With his calculator in hand, he asked questions and we asked him even more questions. In the meantime, my husband excused himself to go to the restroom. That gave me an opportunity to change the conversation, which I felt the Lord was prompting me to do.

I looked at Oscar and said, "You have been so patient and gracious in handling a woman with such specific requests. Thank you for your kindness."

"Well," he said, "I think it's important to allow customers to take their time and have an opportunity to think about how they're spending their hard-earned money." Then he continued, "Besides, I've had two heart attacks and I need to remain calm."

Now, he had my attention, and proceeded to tell me all about his severe heart issues. I couldn't believe what I was hearing. Was this man telling me that he was dying? I tried to speak calmly, but I was really getting concerned, even though we had only met an hour earlier.

He quietly responded, "I've been told there is absolutely *nothing* doctors can do. My arteries are like cement."

By the time he had finished sharing about his health issues and the impossibilities ahead, I felt the gravity of the situation and urgency to ask him *the* question.

Normally, I would hesitate and think, "What will he think if I asked him such a personal question?" However, it didn't even enter my mind. This situation was *too* serious.

He went on to explain how he could have a stroke or drop dead at any time. But he decided he didn't want to sit around at home wondering and waiting. So, he continued to work part-time.

I felt empathy for this man. Then, with deep compassion and with an emphasis on every word, I gently said, "Oscar, may I have your permission to ask you one of the most important questions you'll ever be asked?"

With a surprised look he turned from his calculator and paper work and looked directly at me, responding, "Of course."

I took a deep breath and spoke as slowly and gently as I possibly could, hesitating a little at every phrase. "Oscar… if you died today, do you have any idea where you would spend eternity?"

He hesitated a moment and responded, "Well, I believe that whatever happens, happens. There's nothing I can do about it, so I've decided not to worry. That's why I'm working part time. I've got to keep my mind busy. I know my wife and kids are very concerned, but I keep telling them that there's nothing we can do but accept it."

I wasn't sure if he was skirting around my question or didn't really know how to answer. I just tried to be more specific without being forceful.

So, I asked if he had any spiritual upbringing. He shared that his Armenian father took him to the Greek Orthodox Church on Easter, but that was it. He and his wife didn't attend church either, but he believed in God and he often prayed.

Thoughts raced through my mind like, *where do I begin? How do I explain within seconds about God's plan of salvation?"* I knew time was money for him and I wanted to be sensitive to his work. I briefly explained how God loves him and how He has a plan for his life, whether it is short or many more years to come.

I quickly explained how it's impossible for a person to reach a perfect God because we are all sinners. Thankfully, God sent His Son Jesus to die on a cross and take our sin on Himself. I drew a picture on a page, to help him visualize how the cross bridges the gap between God and man. He was listening to every word as though it may be his only hope.

I continued, "Oscar, the way we can be certain we're going to heaven and spend eternity with God, is by accepting His Son, Jesus Christ, as our personal Lord and Savior. We do it by talking to Him in prayer and asking

Him to forgive us our sins, and then ask Him to come into our heart and life."

His response was, "Well, I think I've led a pretty good life."

How desperately I wanted more time to help him clearly understand, but I knew my time was over and I needed to let him go. I ended with, "You know, I'm glad that you have led a good life. That's more than many can say, but even a good life isn't enough to get us to heaven. We need to ask Jesus to come into our heart and forgive us of our sins. But, when you talk to God, you can tell Him you want to make certain that you will spend eternity with Him."

He looked at me and said, "I don't think your coming was a mistake."

"No," I said, "I marvel how God chose you to help us when we walked through those doors. And because He loves you so much, He wanted you to hear the truth, so that you could be certain where you will spend eternity."

Another customer was waiting for his time and attention so we stood up to walk to the counter and complete the transaction we decided to make.

While he was writing up our purchase, I didn't want this amazing encounter to end. He needed clarity about what we had talked about, so he could ponder and make the most important decision of his life.

As he was writing, I softly spoke so others couldn't hear me, "Oscar, would you be willing to give me your home or email address? I'd like to send you something to explain more clearly, what we've talked about."

He wrote his information on our sales slip, took my hand, looked me in the eyes and said, "Thank you so much. I have really enjoyed our time together." Then, he shook my husband's hand and we all said goodbye.

By the time we got out the door, it was dark outside. We had been in the store for two hours, but it seemed like only minutes.

Suddenly, all the emotion I had been holding back came to the surface. I covered my mouth as I began sobbing, and trying to walk to our car. My heart grieved for this kind man whose life was literally hanging in the balance. I began to pray out loud for him and asked the Lord to spare his life until I could get something sent off to him.

I had one more request for the Lord, I said, "I'm asking You to draw Oscar with your Holy Spirit to see his need for You. And after he invites You into his life, I ask that his life will be so changed that there will be a ripple effect to his wife and children. They need to come to know You too."

I literally felt like we had been standing on holy ground as we talked with this dear man. During the conversation, I had told him we hadn't planned on buying furniture that day, but I was certain God had a purpose for bringing us to his store.

It wasn't until we were driving home, I realized that I had been part of another Divine Appointment. I sat in awe, thinking how the Lord can orchestrate a simple shopping trip into a possible life-changing experience!

UPDATE: A follow-up letter was sent to Oscar the next day. I will never know how he responded. I shared the truth with him and I've trusted God to do the rest.

BAG of POTATOES

When I take the Lord with me, everywhere
I go, things can get really interesting.

I had picked up everything on my grocery list and headed to the check-out line at our neighborhood market. I was minding my own business; however, when I take the Lord with me, I never know what to expect!

The man, waiting in the check-out-line in front of me, was noticeably dirty with straggly hair. He had two other friends with him. They all appeared to be in their 30s. It was obvious they were up to 'No Good,' as my mother would say. They were clearly scheming something and kept whispering back and forth, giving each other a mischievous smile.

I wanted to go to another check-out line but each was longer than the one I was in, so I waited with an uncomfortable sense that something was about to happen.

Inwardly, I started praying, "Lord, please don't ask me to be part of what's going on here. I really don't want to get involved."

After unloading his items on the check-out counter, the man started to reach down and pick up his 20-lb. bag of potatoes from the lower basket of his cart. He hesitated a moment then left them in place and pushed the cart through. He began bagging his own groceries, returning them to the same cart.

It was obvious what he was planning, but I didn't feel comfortable confronting him in front of the other customers.

After the cashier totaled his bill and the man pulled out his food stamps to pay for his groceries, he and his friends quickly walked out through the automatic doors, pushing the grocery cart.

I was thinking, *Lord, that wasn't right, but I don't know what to do.*

As I moved forward to unload my groceries, I softly said to the cashier, "Excuse me ma'am, did you charge that man for the bag of potatoes in the bottom of his cart?"

She panicked and loudly called one of the young workers. "Mark! Run out and stop that guy who has a bag of potatoes in the bottom of his cart. Tell him to come back in and pay for them!"

Then, God began to softly speak into my spirit. I thought, "Lord are you sure?" I knew better than to question because He always has a purpose when He asks me to do something unusual, but seems a bit *crazy* to me.

The cashier completed checking my few items and gave me the final cost. I softly said, "Ma'am, you're probably not going to understand this but God just told me I'm supposed to pay for that man's bag of potatoes." She wrinkled her forehead in a frowning position and slowly said, "Are you sure?" I smiled as I nodded *yes.*

I had no idea what was supposed to happen next but when the man returned, he said to the cashier, "Oh I'm sooo sorry, I guess I must *not* have seen the potatoes. Here," starting to hand her his food stamps, "I'll pay for them now." The checker responded gruffly with an attitude. "No, you don't need to pay! This nice lady already paid for you!"

He turned and gave me the same puzzled response the checker had given me. At that moment, I thought, I'll just let him go and say no more.

Of course, the Lord had a different plan and He whispered in my spirit once again.

As the guy turned to leave, I gently said, "Sir, just a minute." I reached out my hand to shake his dry, weathered, dirty hand and introduced myself. He reluctantly shook mine, saying, "I'm Gary and umm... thanks for paying for my potatoes. I didn't realize I had left them in the bottom of..." I interrupted him as I looked in his eyes and placed my hand firmly around his forearm.

With a dry and nervous throat, I said, "Gary, I've been watching you and you know as well as I do that you lied to the clerk. I watched you and your friends scheming the whole thing." He didn't respond. He just looked stunned and was probably thinking, *where did this weird lady come from and why did she pay for my potatoes?*

I let go of his arm and moved my cart away from the check-out stand. As he followed me, my peripheral vision showed me that the customers and the clerk, were all silent and waiting to see what was going to happen next.

I had Gary's attention and he stood frozen with fear, as though the next thing I might do was tell him every sin he had ever committed. Instead, I said, "Gary, God asked me to pay for those potatoes because He wants me to give you a message. First, He wants you to know how much He loves you." The guy blinked and squinted at me like, *what?*

I continued. "Matter of fact, Gary, He loved you so much that over two thousand years ago, He was hung on a cross to die for the sins of the world. That includes you."

He stood there as though I knew what kind of life he had been living and fear showed in his face.

I knew I had to continue. "You see Gary, my paying for your potatoes was nothing, compared to the high price God's Son, Jesus paid when He gave His life for you on the cross. It was because He loved you, even before you were born. You haven't done anything to deserve His love, but He wants to give you a free gift, the payment He already paid for your sins."

At this point I said, "Let's move outside."

As we left the store, he could have walked away but I'm convinced the Holy Spirit held him in place and he was afraid to move.

I continued, "Gary, you can receive this free gift of love by asking Jesus to forgive you of your sins and by inviting Him into your heart and life. He wants to give you hope and a future"

Gently and caringly, I continued, "God has a plan for your life, but you have been doing your own thing and ignoring Him as He has tugged at your heart. You've been trying to fill the God-shaped vacuum in your life but nothing seems to satisfy. You long to feel whole and complete but everything you do seems to turn out badly. You've tried drugs, alcohol and sex, but nothing satisfies. Gary, Jesus is the longing in your heart. Only He can fill that emptiness."

His buddies were waiting so I told him I would love to share more, but I realized He needed to go. Then I said, "Remember, if you want to see how amazing God is and what He can do in your life, all you need to do is pray a simple prayer, asking for His forgiveness and inviting Him into your heart and life. He longs to have a relationship with you. You can talk to Him about anything, just like you're talking with me."

I told him I would be praying for him. Then, before he left, he reached out his hand once again. This time, he graciously thanked me for my kindness and for the things I had shared.

As he walked away, I took a deep breath and thought, *Did I say what the Lord wanted me to say?* I felt like I really bungled it up but I had to trust the Lord with the whole amazing situation. It was only the Lord who could have given me the ability to even talk, because on the inside, I was trembling throughout my whole body.

After I placed my groceries in the trunk of my car and got situated in the driver's seat, I put my head down and tears started to flow.

I prayed, *Oh Lord, forgive me for not wanting to get involved. I know, you had that Divine Appointment planned and all I needed to do was listen as you spoke in my spirit. Please help Gary to remember the words you gave him, through me. I pray that your Holy Spirit will awaken him even in the middle of the night and remind him of your great love for him. Bring him to the place where he surrenders his life to You.*

When I arrived home, I thought about the inner struggle I had experienced earlier that morning, when the Lord was asking me to spend time with Him. But instead, I chose to run out the door.

I knew I should have taken time to get alone with Him, but I felt rushed because I had a long list of things to accomplish. Then, before I closed the front door behind me, I heard two words softly slip into my spirit. *"Seek First,"* it whispered.

I knew what it meant. I had read Matthew 6:33 many times. He was calling me and I wanted to honor His call to place Him first in my day.

So instead of going forward with my list of things to do, I went back inside, took my coat off, put the car keys on the table, sat down and said, "I don't know how I'm going to get everything done today, but Lord, I give my plans to you and ask you to quiet my heart as I choose to take this time to spend alone with you."

I was so grateful I had met with Jesus that morning because it was amazing how He gave me the words to speak to an absolute stranger. I would have really been a mess if I hadn't given Him the first part of my day. And, I would have missed the most important appointment He chose for my day.

MY WHITE HAIR

It's fascinating how God can use an electronic malfunction to fulfill His purpose.

We had spent the night at a hotel on our way north from California to Southern Oregon. My husband's elderly parents' health was failing, and we felt it necessary to spend a few days with them, to make certain they were getting the best care possible, while in assisted living.

Most hotels have a free breakfast, though I don't particularly care for their unhealthy choices of powdered eggs, white-floured pancakes with fake syrup.

My new doctor made it clear as to the diet we should follow. So, I asked my husband if we could find a restaurant where I could order fresh scrambled eggs to go. I needed something healthier to take with my supplements. He was understanding and we found the perfect restaurant.

He dropped me off to order my soft-scrambled-eggs, while he went to Starbucks to pick up a Vanilla Latte. As I stood at the counter waiting for my eggs, I heard a woman's voice behind me, saying, "Ma'am, I love your beautiful white hair."

Every time I hear that compliment, I am shocked because I have lost half my hair, due to a low thyroid, and, I've had to learn some tricks to cause it to look fuller. So. when people compliment me on my hair, I say, "Thank you," and then I'd think, *if they only knew the extensive process I go through.*

I turned around and saw an older woman sitting at the restaurant booth with another woman, a few years younger. I responded, "Are you talking to me?" Her response was, "Well, of course I am!" And with an insistent voice, she said, "Come here!"

I walked over to her table and she took hold of my arm, not letting me go. I really was anxious to get my eggs and be on my way, but she didn't seem to care about my schedule. (Thankfully, she didn't frighten me by her boldness. I'm used to unusual people.)

When my eggs arrived, the older lady moved over and invited me to sit down. I learned her name was June and her sister, 12 years younger, was sitting across from her.

I was trying to concentrate on our conversation but in the back of my mind, I was thinking, w*hy is Craig taking so long?* With each question from her, I became more certain that the Holy Spirit was guiding the conversation and He had a purpose in our meeting. With that in mind, I realized I'd better cool my jets and eat my eggs.

I turned to the woman and asked her age. "Eighty-five," she proudly reported. I knew what I needed to ask her next but I never expected such a weird question would come out of my mouth. I asked, "How old do you think you will be when you die?" I was amazed she wasn't embarrassed by my question. Instead, she quickly came back with, "I don't have a clue! I tell you, honey, I hope I don't have to wait very much longer because I'm done with this old world. I'd like out!"

That's all I needed to hear! A response like that troubles me and always leads me to the same question. So, I asked, "June, I'm going to ask you the most important question you probably have ever been asked." I hesitated for a moment to see her response. She appeared anxious to hear what I was going to say, so I slowly and clearly continued. "If you died today, do you know where you would spend eternity?"

Every time I ask that question, I think, *is she going to think I'm a fool and tell me it's none of my business?"*

Instead, I was surprised with her quick response. "Well, I hope I will go to be with Jesus Christ." That response told me that she had a Christian influence in her life. If a person knows nothing about Jesus, they usually say that they've tried to live a good life, so they hope they will be accepted into heaven.

Or, they tell me they've gone to church most of their life. I was so grateful I didn't have to explain how trying to live a good life or going to church is not the ticket to spending eternity in heaven with God.

Although making positive choices and going to church are beneficial, God's Word (The Bible) clearly shows us how we can be certain He will allow us into eternity with Him.

June went on to explain how she had lived a horrible life and had made some really bad choices in years past. Her sister chimed in, "You're not kidding you made bad choices. I'm here to confirm that to be true!"

I didn't want her sister to speak unkindly, even if it was the truth.

I restated her words. "June, you feel you have made wrong choices and you feel badly about the things you have done in your past...right?" She shook her head yes, so I continued. "May I ask, if you have ever asked Jesus to forgive you of your sins?" Again, no hesitation or trying to remember what response she should give. Immediately, she said, "Yes I have." I told her that, *"If we confess our sins, He is faithful and just to forgive us our sins and will cleanse us from all unrighteousness."* (I John 1:9)

June looked at me with amazement. It was clear she had carried the weight of her past wrong-choices for many years. I assured her that God loved her and when we ask forgiveness, He no longer will remember our sins because the Bible says, *He will bury them in the sea of forgetfulness.* (Micah 7:19, my shortened translation).

As I looked out the window, I saw my husband drive into the parking lot. I thought, *but Lord, I have so much more I need to share with her.* I told June and her sister that I would love to talk more but my husband had arrived and we had a long trip ahead.

As I stood up to go, June grabbed my hand and said, "Karen, will you please pray with us before you leave?" I agreed and as I prayed, I asked for God's blessing on both women, thanking Him for bringing us together for that short time.

Although I wanted more time, I could trust that God would follow up where I had left off.

Before I turned to leave, I said, "If I don't see you again, I will look for you when we all get to heaven." I hugged them both and said, "Good bye."

As I returned to the car I prayed, "Lord, that was a Divine Appointment orchestrated only by You! Now I understand why You brought me together with June and her sister." She had been living in condemnation and needed to hear truth spoken to her, and receive new freedom in Jesus.

I realized, once again, He wanted to show His love to June because He cares about each detail of our lives. And, in this situation, He wanted June to know that she is truly forgiven! What a love gift to her. The joy in her eyes, after our conversation, was evident! "Thank you, Lord."

When I returned to the car, my husband said, "Boy there was a long line at Starbucks! The computer system had broken down and it seemed to take forever! Thankfully, I got a free latte' out of it because I had to wait so long."

I laughed, "It wasn't the long line that held you up. It was the Lord! Being late gave me just enough time to finish what He had planned for me to share with two older women."

Isn't God amazing? He used my white hair to begin that priceless conversation! And then He delayed my husband at Starbucks with the electronic malfunction, until I finished the words He had for me to share!

His faithfulness blesses me every time He orchestrates a *new* Divine Appointment.

ASPEN with NO HORSERADISH

With a grin, he responded,
"Yes, and mine had horseradish."

One day in the middle of December, I had a list of errands to run. I wasn't feeling well, so I postponed my plans. Thankfully, I felt better the next day, allowing me to grab my list and head off to complete my errands.

By 4pm, I realized I hadn't eaten since early that morning and my stomach was growling with a, *please feed me* kind of growl.

As I drew close to my favorite bakery and sandwich shop, Aspen Mills, I remembered my husband wouldn't be home for dinner. It was a perfect opportunity to stop and order my favorite sandwich to take home and enjoy.

After I placed my order, an Aspen with *no* horseradish, I walked around viewing all the fresh baked goodies, until I heard my name, "Karen." I walked up to the counter and the lady said, "Aspen with *no* horseradish?" I had previously paid, so I thanked her and turned to walk out with my small white lunch sack, containing the sandwich, dill pickle, and small potato salad. My mouth was watering.

I heard a young man's voice behind me saying, "Oh, I got an Aspen sandwich, too, but mine *does* have horseradish." There were no other customers so I figured the guy was mumbling to himself. He continued chatting about his delightful sandwich as I walked out the door, with him following me.

As though I was listening, he said, "I haven't had bread for months because I shouldn't be eating it, but I was so hungry for my favorite sandwich, I just had to stop."

I continued to walk straight ahead as he continued chatting, "I had chemo today and am weak but I'm so hungry." I had been thinking, *you are talking to me because why? Do I even know you?* However, when the word, *chemo* registered in my brain, he had my attention!

I stopped abruptly and slowly turned around to look at the young man more directly. With a voice of compassion, which only the Lord could have given, I said, "May I ask what kind of illness you have?"

His weak voice quivered, "Leukemia and Myelofibrosis, a rare bone-marrow cancer which is normally an incurable disease."

He continued, "I've been told I have 1½ years, at the most." His skin color was very jaundiced and he looked like he wouldn't last much longer.

Deep compassion tugged at my heart and his voice broke as he tried to talk. Tears kept softly spilling down his cheeks. His voice cracked and his raw emotions clearly validated that he needed someone to listen.

My first thought was, *this man cannot die without knowing Christ*! I knew I had to ask!

Without hesitation, I said, "You've only just met me, but I feel I need to ask you the most important question you'll ever be asked."

I paused a moment and then gently said, "Do you have any idea where you will spend eternity when it's your time to leave this earth?"

Usually, in situations like this, I hear one of these responses: "No"… or…"I'm not really sure, but I hope I'll go to heaven,"…or…"I've tried to live a good life; of course I'm not perfect, but I hope God will let me in."

Although I was shocked, I was delighted when he responded with a clear and definitive, "Yes, I have accepted Jesus Christ as my Lord and Savior!"

He went on to tell me that it all started seven months previously when he looked in the mirror one morning. He was shocked to see how yellow his skin appeared. Realizing he was in trouble he went straight to emergency.

After the diagnosis, his life totally changed. It became more serious, contemplative, and focused on Jesus.

Due to the advanced disease in his body, life took on new meaning. His previous interests were in cars, women, and anything exciting in this world. Now, they were no longer attractive to him.

The tears continued to come as we talked. When he mentioned the name of Jesus, he talked as though he had a personal relationship with Him. Yet, he also expressed the fear he had because even though the Lord had forgiven him of his past sinful lifestyle, he was still concerned there was a possibility God might reject him when he dies. He said he wasn't fearful of dying, but he *was* afraid of rejection and being consumed by darkness as he stepped into eternity. He couldn't handle the thought of God turning His back on him.

I never dreamed I would be sharing information about how Satan uses crafty lies and deception to make us believe wrong thoughts.

Standing there, only feet away from the bakery's door, hungry and holding our white sandwich bags, I was grateful no other customers were walking by.

I sensed the Holy Spirit take over as I began to share answers to his concerns. I told him he didn't need to feel worried or condemned because Romans 8:1 tells us that *if we are in Christ Jesus* (not living according to the flesh but according to the Spirit), *we are covered by the blood of*

Jesus that was shed at Calvary. And, when we ask His forgiveness for our sins and thank Him for dying on the cross for us, John 3:16 clearly shows us that we will not perish but have everlasting life with Him! That means He *will* accept us as we step into eternity.

I continued, "His acceptance of us is not because of trying to live a good life. There is no way a perfect God could accept us because of anything *we* do. It's all about *Jesus*. When we invite Him into our heart and life, He shows His amazing love, and He accepts us into His family. We are covered with His blood that washes us whiter than snow." (Psalm 51:7)

What a sight we were. I was old enough to be his mother, but he didn't seem to care. He kept thanking me for being willing to listen to him. He had been carrying a heavy burden and concern, knowing he could die sooner than later, and the uncertainty about whether or not he had done enough to be accepted by God.

At that moment, I knew God had orchestrated our plans to meet at Aspen Mills. I took our conversation in a different direction by asking if he had ever been prayed for? His response was, "Yes, two nurses prayed for me in the hospital." I thought wow, *thank you Lord for those bold nurses who are compassionate with their patients and care for them physically and spiritually.*

I smiled at him as I said, "Do you realize that we've talked all this time and I don't even know your name?" I could tell he was getting very tired, but he looked into my eyes and softly smiled, saying, "My name is Dan." Because he was young enough to be my son, I thought about my own son having to go through health issues like Dan. I said, "Dan, my name is Karen. I am so thankful the Lord brought us to the same bakery at the same time to each buy an Aspen sandwich."

With a grin he responded, "Yes, and mine *had* horseradish."

I realized, if I had pushed myself to run out and do my list of errands the day before, when I didn't feel well, I would have missed this amazing Divine Appointment with Dan. After this realization, I thanked the Lord for the pain that kept me home, until *He* was ready to invite me to partner with Him in Dan's life.

HIS STORY CONTINUES

Only God knows the day or the hour
any of us will step into eternity.

One thing I have learned through all these assignments is that God is the Author of each of the stories of our lives.

Sometimes stories have a definite beginning, middle, and end. Other times, stories may linger on without an obvious ending.

This is a continuation of the previous story about Dan's life.

Dan moved from California to New York some months after we met, to be near family. We kept in touch by occasionally texting.

When I originally met Dan, he was needing blood transfusions on a regular basis. Then, soon after we started praying for him, he experienced over 500 days without needing one blood transfusion. That alone was a miracle!

His faith was strong and he never allowed negative words to be spoken. He must have been familiar with Proverbs 18:21 that reminds us how we have the power to speak words of life or death over ourselves. He chose life!

Then, in July of 2020 I received a call from him. He was calling his close friends and kept the calls short and to the point. The doctor had just told him that, at the most, he had no more than 5 days remaining.

It was difficult for him to talk because of his emotions but he thanked me for all my prayer support, and we said good bye. I didn't believe it was his time to pass but I also believed the doctor. *Wrong choice!*

It looked like his next really big miracle would be stepping into eternity and spending forever with, as he called Him, *Sweet Jesus*, the One he so deeply loved.

Five days passed and when I opened my cell phone on the 6th day, I was shocked to see a selfie from Dan! What? I felt like a fool for believing the doctor!

I gave up on the doctor's prognosis and quickly texted back, "OK! Now I'm really going to hold on for a miracle!"

In time, he changed his way of thinking and praying. I had told him how there is **power in praise**. So, he began thanking God for his healing and I did the same.

However, in October of 2020, I received a text saying, "JESUS is calling me home, my friend." I quickly returned a text saying, "How do you know?" His abbreviated response said, "U know… in hosp."

Well, I've never died before, so who was I not to believe what he was experiencing. However, I still didn't sense it was his time to pass. I was holding on for a miracle!

I later learned that he had a serious blood infection and they had given him 5 bags of blood. After that news, there were no more texts. Almost a month went by.

During this time of silence, my husband and I prayed for him every day.

Then I said, "Honey, I don't think Dan is with us anymore. I'm surprised his sister hasn't notified us. I then asked myself, *was I like the person in James 1:6-8, believing for a miracle one moment but with weak faith the next?*

When my husband told me to text Dan's phone, I said…

> "What good would that do? He can't
> text me back from Heaven!"

Now, although I was certain Dan was with Jesus, I took Craig's suggestion and texted the words, "Dan, how are you doing?"

The next day, I received a text, saying, "Hi Karen."

I figured it was his sister responding, but instead, it was Dan…he was alive!!

I read his 7 brief cryptic texts, telling me he had been in the hospital for 13 days and he *almost* died. It was a blood infection.

After that news, there were no more texts for several weeks…again.

December arrived and a text finally came with three praying-hands emojis. This turned out to be his way of communicating with me.

Ok, he was still alive.

Two weeks later he again texted me with his typical symbol response, but this time he added three powerful words: "Praise Sweet JESUS!" I knew that phrase belonged to Dan.

The roller coaster of wondering if he had passed, but the hope that he was still holding on and expecting his big miracle, was beginning to wear me down emotionally.

I decided the only way God wanted me to think was to believe that Dan was already healed. Jesus took the beating and the deep and painful stripes on His back for Dan's victorious healing over cancer, over 2000 years ago.

Why is it that we can believe that Jesus died for our sins but many don't believe He also paid the price for our healing today?

Perhaps God was waiting for my faith to truly believe that he was already healed, and now Dan is waiting for his symptoms to leave.

Yes, Jesus still heals today! And, I believe this for Dan! I pray it comes **quickly**!

UPDATE: It has been two years since I *first* met Dan. He has gone through many near-death experiences but continues to trust God's plan for his life. In his weakness, he occasionally sends me his three pairs of *praying-hands* emojis. It's as if he wants me to know he is still alive, and he's asking me to continue praying for him.

As of this writing, Dan is still with us.

I'm holding on for a MIRACLE!

BLACK BEAR DINER

Jesus, how can I partner with Your
Spirit as I go through my day?

We had been traveling all summer, leaving the California heat for Oregon and Washington. Now, it was September – time to return to our small condo in Palm Springs.

After leaving Jacksonville, our favorite little town in southern Oregon, we drove to Redding, California for a late breakfast at the Black Bear Restaurant.

While traveling, we had been listening to a book, entitled *Experiencing God,* by Henry Blackaby. The author spoke words that impacted my thoughts when he encouraged the reader to ask the Lord how we can partner with God's Spirit as we go through our day.

So, immediately I said, "Lord, how can I partner with what You want to do through me, even as we go into this restaurant?" I wanted the Lord to know I was willing to be available for whatever He desired.

Prior to being seated at our table, my thoughts were distracted by a text I had just received only minutes before. My friend was traveling and had become very sick.

She needed prayer. After placing our order, we took a moment to pray for her and to cover her with God's healing power. (Yes, I believe God still heals today. I have personally had 5 miraculous healings in my body.)

Throughout our meal, my thoughts were for my friend's needs, not on the earlier prayer of, 'How can I partner with you Lord.' I'm glad God knew my heart.

Moments later, a kind-looking man, probably in his 30's, and his approximately 3-year old son entered the restaurant. As this young father was talking to the hostess, his young son was steps away, pushing buttons on an old jukebox that everyone else passed without noticing. This young boy had noticed because the buttons were at his eye level.

In seconds, the dad turned around and touched the child. As the boy looked up, he saw the big smile from his daddy's face. It appeared to say, *Isn't it fun to push those buttons?* Then, I heard him gently say, "OK son, let's go have lunch."

The hostess led the man and his boy to a booth, directly on the other side of where we were sitting, with a 4' high wooden divider separating us. She handed him a menu, a printed paper and crayons for the child. Within moments, dad was sitting there coloring, right along with his son. It was precious to watch their interaction.

This was so different than when I've seen dads do at a restaurant with their children. Usually, the dad is on his phone and the kids are being ignored. So many parents miss opportunities to really connect with their children.

As I was observing this father and his son, something started to stir in my spirit. I heard the still small voice of the Lord, saying, *tell him he is doing a great job as a dad.*

Sure, I didn't hear an actual voice, but when an impression from God touches my spirit it's like an audible voice.

Sometimes, if I have time to think about what God has spoken, I question if it is really Him. I wondered what this young man would think of a stranger, an older woman, boldly talking to him? Would he even care what I would have to say?

I continued to wrestle with my thoughts until I realized what was happening. Yup! Satan was hot on my trail and trying to mess with my mind. If you don't believe me, choose to obey God in a situation where He has asked you to do something difficult. Believe me, Satan does **not** want you to obey God, or to be a blessing to another person. He will often make you doubt and second-guess yourself about what you believe God is asking you to do.

After finishing our meal, my husband, who didn't know what was going on in my mind, because we had been talking about other things, said, "Are you ready to go?"

He got up to go to the cashier. I hesitated. Should I deliver the message to this stranger, or should I just let it go? Why was I still questioning?

Do you have any idea how many times I've struggled with this same question? I know the Lord is patient but I didn't want to refuse His request. I thought, *what harm would it actually do to encourage someone?* Besides, the times I didn't respond, I was miserable afterward. So, I knew I would regret it if I didn't partner with my Lord.

I said, "Holy Spirit, please speak through me." Then, I slowly stood up and turned towards the young man. I leaned forward on my bench seat and gently said, "Excuse me sir."

He looked up at me and waited to hear what I had to say.

"You may think I'm crazy…. but God just spoke a message into my spirit…for you."

The man remained quiet, waiting with expectancy for the punch line.

I continued, using gentle expressions and looking into his eyes, slowly and gently emphasizing the words God had given me. *"God wants me to tell you that…you are doing a great job as a Dad!"* I gave the word "great" the most loving and fervent emphasis possible.

Then I thought, "Wow God, thank you for taking over. I could never have delivered that short message so lovingly."

The young man gave me a really big, satisfying smile and a genuine and appreciative, "Thank you!" He looked as though he was hoping I had more to say but I said only what God had asked me to say. I know that short positive phrase blessed and touched him deep in his spirit.

Well, I did it!

Did I bless him or harm him by interrupting his time with his son? I could have ignored God's voice but I remembered a quote I heard once: *If we choose not to listen to God's gentle voice, He will eventually stop speaking to us.*

I don't want Him to stop speaking to me. My prayer is that when He speaks, I won't even question. I want to listen and obey His first request.

When my grandchildren were young, I used to sing a little song that was based on a really old chorus but I changed a couple of words. I often used it when they didn't listen the first time and obey. It went like this…

Listen and Obey, for there's no other way, to be happy in the fam-i-ly… but to Listen and Obey.

If I want to be happy in my relationship with Jesus, *listening* to His voice and obeying what He asks of me, is not only the best way to respond, it's the only way! That means, trusting my Lord in whatever He asks of me, no matter how humbling the situation might be.

Each time I DO choose to obey, an amazing JOY floods into my heart! That makes it worth it all!

As I left the restaurant, in my spirit I thought, *thank you Lord for allowing me one more* opportunity to *partner with You*...and *bless that young father.*

KOREAN STUDENTS

What did I get myself into?

I was asked to speak to a group of Korean students who had been invited by Desert Chapel Christian School in Palm Springs, CA.

They would each live in a host's home for one month and would take classes with the American students from the school. They had studied English in Korea and wanted to practice English while living in the United States.

About 15 students were expected, ages 14-16, and the class would take place during the last period of the day. Their teacher from Korea was expected to attend with them. I was surprised to learn that I had the freedom to choose any topic I wanted to speak on, and I would have a full hour.

Any topic?

I thought, *Then I will tell a brief story of my life, including how I came to know Jesus and how He has changed my life.* I planned on drawing stick figures on the white board to illustrate everything I was talking about; and I would speak slowly just in case they had difficulty understanding my English.

I was thrilled to take this assignment and felt comfortable with any age because I had experience with all grades, K-12, from my training in Education.

That said, I felt the most important preparation was **prayer**. Before I went into the classroom, I asked the Holy Spirit to go before me and speak through me.

After arriving early and getting prepared to meet with the students, I expected they would probably be reserved, respectful and gracious. Instead, 15 Korean teenagers walked into the room behaving noisily and ignoring the lady standing in the front of the class. They were all jabbering in Korean and I thought, *what did I get myself into? How am I ever going to get their attention?*

I began praying again in my thoughts, *Jesus, I can't do this, but I invite You to be the teacher today. Please take over and speak through me.* As my quick prayer ended, the bell rang.

Competing over their noise, I spoke loudly and slowly, saying, "Thank you for taking your seats and being good listeners." They quieted down and 1 continued in my normal calm voice. "I have something to tell you that you may never have heard before. I'm going to tell you about an amazing man who can totally change your life."

I had their attention and even the girl in the front row, who had been showing off and trying desperately to get everyone's attention, calmed down and listened. Then, within a few minutes, when she realized she had been too quiet, she returned to her obnoxious behavior. As she chattered away in Korean, I stepped closer and gently touched her arm as I continued talking and looking around at all the other students. Immediately, she fell silent.

I started introducing myself by writing my name on the whiteboard. I then told them my age. In unison, they all said, "WOW!" It sounded like they thought my age was ancient! And, when I told them I had been married twice, they gasped like I had done something very shameful.

By this time, I was laughing inside, but I continued to explain that my first husband had died in the Vietnam War, and I had remarried 4 years later. They seemed to think that was fine. Thankfully, they were listening and following every word I shared.

After the short overview of my life, I moved into my talk about Jesus. With drawings on the whiteboard, I explained God, Jesus and the Holy Spirit. They were absolutely silent. I explained about the birth of Jesus, His death and how He rose from the dead on the third day.

Their expressions showed their surprise and realization that they had never heard this story before; but they were captivated by what I had shared.

Now, keep in mind, I was trying to cover everything I thought was important, but I had to talk slowly and explain things in detail.

At one point the Korean teacher came in and apologized that she had gotten tied up and couldn't be with us. I was actually delighted she had not been available because I wanted to feel the freedom to share whatever I felt led to say. I graciously told her I had a teaching degree and we were doing just fine; she could feel free to do whatever she needed to do. Thankfully, she left.

When I came to the part where I shared how I spend time with Jesus each morning, I noticed the restless girl, in the front row, had tears running down her cheeks. These 15 kids were obviously not the same individuals who had walked in earlier.

Now they were silent and hungry for every word that was being shared. There was no other explanation. The Holy Spirit had filled every inch of that classroom.

The hour passed so quickly and my talk was finished. Before I excused them, I prayed over them. And as I said, "Amen," the bell rang.

I stood there waiting but no one moved. I said, "The bell rang and you may go, if you would like. School is over." They silently remained in their seats. I thought, certainly they had heard the bell, but now I assumed that the Lord had more in mind.

I asked, "What do you like best about being in the United States?" No one responded. Then I said, "What do you like most about being at this school?" A 16-year-old boy raised his hand immediately and said, "I like this." I didn't understand what he was saying so I asked him to explain. In his simple English he said, "I like you talk about Jesus." His eyes were tearing. I realized God was doing something precious with each of these teenage Korean students.

Slowly and clearly, I asked if anyone would like to have a relationship with Jesus by inviting Him into their heart and life. I was **shocked**!

Did they really understand what I was asking? All they could say was, "We hear more?"

Earlier, in my presentation, I had shared how much God loved them and how His Son died on the cross for their sins. Now, the invitation was to ask Jesus to forgive them of their sins and invite Him into their hearts and lives. Once again, I explained what it meant to have a relationship with Him, and if that was what they wanted, we just talk to Jesus in prayer.

I told them I would say a prayer and if they wanted to repeat it after me, they could. Or, if they wanted to leave… that was o.k. too.

No one left.

So, I asked them to bow their heads and close their eyes, and repeat after me.

Speaking in short phrases, I said:

"Dear Jesus,

Thank You for loving me.

Thank You for dying on the cross for my sins.

Forgive me for all the wrong things I have done.

Please come into my heart and life.

I know You live in heaven with God,

but thank You that Your Holy Spirit will always be with me.

Someday, when I die, I want to live with You forever. Amen"

This wasn't the typical prayer I would normally use, but that's what came out of my mouth. As I looked around at the students, I was amazed because they seemed to understand what they had just done. I felt I could have literally cut the PEACE that filled that room with a knife, because it was so thick.

I didn't know how many prayed with me, but that was in God's hands.

I had explained that praying that prayer would mean they desired to become a follower of Jesus Christ, and they seemed thrilled! I encouraged them to get a Korean Bible and start reading in the Book of John.

As they walked out of the room, their countenance was different. They thanked me over and over for everything I had shared.

I was stunned by their response. It certainly wasn't my presentation alone. The Lord brought His Holy Spirit into that classroom and drew the hearts of those teenagers to Himself. It was precious to watch.

Afterwards, I chatted with the 16-year-old boy who said he liked talking about Jesus. The thought came to me that *someday that boy may be an evangelist in Korea, sharing the Good News about his Savior. Only God knows how many people he will lead to Christ when he returns home.*

The Holy Spirit had shown up and took over in an awesome way. What a joy it was to partner with Jesus in that classroom!

SHE NODDED

God had done what looked to be impossible.

I unexpectedly received a text informing me that a woman named *Patti* had been admitted into a hospital. The text explained that a feeding tube was inserted and a colostomy was performed.

As the text continued, I thought, w*ho is this person who is texting such personal information?* So, I responded, "I would appreciate knowing who the writer of this text is. Your phone number is not in my contact list."

It turned out to be my husband's only male cousin, Jim, texting me about his wife's health condition. I was surprised because this was the first time he had ever contacted me! Perhaps my cell number was in Patti's phone.

The many years I had known Patti, she had dealt with Multiple Sclerosis and had been in a wheel chair a great deal of that time. Later she became bed-ridden.

When I learned she was now in critical condition, I was deeply concerned. The text stated she had been hospitalized about 115 miles away from their home. She also had several additional health concerns. I knew her diagnosis was very grim. The thought came to my mind, *God! Please don't let her die. I'm not sure she is ready to meet You.*

After the initial contact, his texts included nothing but bad news; she underwent a stomach surgery that resulted in several severe complications.

One of the texts I sent, said, "Jim, this may not make any sense to you, but I am deeply concerned for Patti. All I know is that when God places a heaviness on my heart for someone, I know He's asking me to be devoted in prayer for them. I believe He's asking me to stand in the gap for Patti."

After the last surgery, the doctor informed Jim that Patti had a twisted gut and she would not have survived without surgery; it was unrelated to any previous procedures. The fact that they *found* that particular problem was answered prayer! But the fact that she *lived through* the procedure was an even bigger result of prayer!

The Lord continued to awaken me at all hours of the night. I always knew He was inviting me to pray for Patti. Then, one night as I was praying, a quietness swept over me. Suddenly, God gave me a spiritual vision. (It's like watching a video the Lord gives for a specific reason.)

In the vision, I was standing next to Patti on her right side in a hospital room. I gently placed my left hand on her forehead and my right hand over her heart and softly began to speak to her: "Patti, you may be dying, but I've asked God not to allow you to slip into eternity until you have an opportunity to receive Jesus as your personal Savior. I know you can't speak but I believe you can hear me. If you would like to pray, just repeat this prayer after me, in your thoughts:

Dear Jesus... Please forgive me for the sin in my life...come into my heart...I want to be forever with You in heaven... Amen.

In the vision, I hesitated after each phrase, allowing her time to speak the words in her thoughts.

Then, the vision ended. I knew this was a confirmation that God was in agreement with my heart for her. It was a precious and humbling experience for me.

God placed a certainty in my spirit that she would not die, even though the medical evidence told otherwise. I felt so certain; I texted a verse to Jim. I told him that Jeremiah 29:11 was for Patti:

"For I know the plans I have for you, declares the Lord, plans to prosper you (in health) and not to harm you, plans to give you a hope and a future."

There was another surgery shortly after the last one. She was so weak, I told my husband, "I have never been called by God to pray for anyone like I have been called for Patti." I felt like I was literally in a war against the forces of darkness. I was exhausted, but I truly believed God had a plan for her and would not allow her to be taken from this earth until He had completed His will for her life.

Jim's texts sounded like she was getting close to passing, so I quickly texted him, "Jim, I want Patti to clearly understand that she has a choice, if she wants to spend eternity with God, all she needs to say is… *Jesus, I need you. Please forgive me for any sin in my life. Thank you for dying on the cross for me. I want to spend eternity in heaven with you.*"

I continued, "By not accepting Jesus as her Savior would mean eternal separation from God. The pain she has experienced on this earth, would not compare to the severity of what she would face without Jesus."

I wanted Jim to understand it wasn't about following a religion or attending a specific church. It's about a relationship with Jesus. I also explained that when God's Spirit enters our spirit, He makes everything new. I finally ended with, "Jim, it's so simple, and God is so amazing!"

In a very short time, things worsened, and the doctor discovered infections around her heart and other areas in her body. She was too weak for another surgery. And, now she was unconscious and remained on a ventilator for oxygen.

I was so broken by the news that we cancelled the meeting we had planned on attending that evening. Instead, PRAYER was the most important thing on our agenda!

In time, I received another text from Jim, saying that Patti was awake! I thought, *What! Awake*? I quickly sent him a short text saying, "Can you talk to her?" His response took me to my knees. He said, "Yes, and I read to her what you said about asking Jesus to save her."

By this time, I was sobbing, with tears. All I could think was, s*he is alive and she now knows the choice she has before her."* Then I thought*, but Lord, she can't talk. She has tubes everywhere!*

I quickly texted Jim again. "Do you feel Patti understood the text that you read to her? Did she accept it for herself?" He responded. "I believe so …SHE NODDED."

I never realized how a simple word like *nodded* could have such amazing meaning! I ran into my husband's office, crying and trying to talk. "Honey, she nodded…she nodded!" He calmly responded, "Who nodded?" In my emotional state, I tried to explain what had happened. Then we both wept joyous tears together. *God had done what looked to be impossible!*

Although the doctor had prepared Jim for the possibility of her death, they also added that no matter what happened, she would never be able to go back to their home as she had requested.

Then, as if it couldn't have gotten any worse, I received word that she was taken in for *still* another procedure. This time, they found abscesses in other organs with fluid build-up in her lungs and chest cavity. Drainage tubes were added. Patti was in an absolutely dire condition.

The information was never consistent because God was still at work in Patti, this side of heaven.

I should never have been surprised when the next text arrived saying, "If the antibiotics are working, we will try to take her home so that she can die there. The doctor figured she had about a 1% chance of getting to go home." Jim ended with, "*It's in God's Hands!*" I was amazed by his response. I had *never* heard him talk about God before.

He drove the 100+ miles home for a quick rest and when he called the hospital, the word was that she was slowly getting stronger. The ventilator was still in but she was mostly breathing on her own.

I did a happy dance, knowing God
was doing something amazing!

When Jim returned to the hospital, he noticed she was more alert and his texts to me sounded more encouraging. Of course, he realized she was still labeled *terminal*; and, he knew he needed to accept it.

Then two days later, the new text read, "Ventilator tube is out! She can talk and laugh. Looking good. Next stop is home, when white blood cell count is normal." Each text gave us new direction in prayer. Now we focused on her white blood count.

It all happened so quickly. The hospital made the arrangements and in a few days the message read, *Medical Transport will be taking her home!*

I cried tears of joy when I read, "She is home… happy, alert, and cheerful! She is noticeably stronger." We were overjoyed and praising God!

Daily, she grew stronger and each text continued to bring additional positive reports!

This experience showed us that there definitely is a place for doctors, but life isn't over until GOD says it's over! He loved Patti so much that He gave her the opportunity to accept Him into her life and then gave her over 4-½ extra years, after the doctor told her she only had 1% chance to survive.

One day God called her home to live with Him for eternity. If she could speak to us, I know she would say,

"Ohhh, that was a blessed day when I got to see Jesus. I can't wait for you to see how wonderful it is here. The Love, Peace and Joy is so amazing. And, the music the angels sing, is like nothing you have ever experienced. I'll be sure to greet you at the gate when it's your time to join me. I love you all."

REST STOP

*What if she was an angel who
had been planted there by God?*

We had left Seattle early in the morning, heading to southern Oregon to visit my husband's elderly parents.

When we travel, my husband is used to me saying, "Let's stop at the next rest-stop so I can go potty." However, he mentioned a new rest-stop a few miles further down the road and wondered if I could wait. I said, "Yes, I think I'm okay." Then, just before the turn-off, I changed my mind. I thought, "Why did I say that? I could have waited until the next rest stop."

When we pulled up to park, I observed an uncomfortable situation that I normally would want to avoid. God might ask me to get involved, and I wasn't interested because we had a long trip ahead.

I could see that a young woman was leaning with her back against a building, holding a cardboard sign that read, "Family of 7 in bind. Need help'" This was a new twist – a needy person standing at a rest stop.

You've got to understand, I don't think that I have the gift of mercy or compassion, so I don't naturally feel a strong emotional pull to help people. However, when He wants me to respond to someone in need, He clearly shows me if I should; then He gives me the grace to lovingly respond with compassion.

If I see a guy standing on the street corner in our home town, with his cardboard sign and a compelling message, I usually don't feel drawn to help; especially since I heard a TV news program that reported the average income of these people comes to about $60,000. Wow!

In this situation, I did NOT feel drawn to help this pitiful-looking woman who held her sign, with her head hanging down, looking at the cement beneath her.

I walked to the restroom and said nothing. Then the thought came, *what if she was an angel who had been planted there by God?* I had heard of other stories of encounters with angels, but I didn't entertain the thought.

After I had finished and washed my hands, I started to walk to the car, but it was like I was being guided to walk right over to the lady.

A gentle boldness and compassion came over me. When I reached her, I said, "Would you be willing to share what your situation is and what your need is?" I had **not** planned on talking to her, but the Holy Spirit redirected my steps.

She slowly raised her head and her weary eyes met mine.

She responded, "We had an Adult Family Home and had several problems. We kept going into more and more debt until we had to close it down. Now, we are left with a lot of debt, no money, and we're living in that old motor home. She pointed behind me and I turned to look. She was right. It was old and didn't appear to even be drivable.

The scene was oppressive.

I quickly changed the topic. Have you had anything to eat today?" I asked. "Yes," she responded, "I had a granola bar." I continued, "Could you use a little fruit? My husband and I are traveling and I have some left over from lunch." All I had offered was fruit, but her eyes lit up like she had not tasted fruit in years. Humbly, she said, "I will gratefully take anything."

My husband had been standing by the side of our car waiting and I thought he might be thinking, *Oh boy, there's my wife, talking to another stranger again!* Instead, he told me that he was wondering how she was responding and if she was really legit (for real).

When I was in the restroom, I too, was wondering, so I said, "Lord, show me through your Holy Spirit if she has a real need. And if she does, show us how to respond. Otherwise, make it clear if she doesn't."

I have learned that if my spirit feels troubled, I would say, "I'm sorry, I can't help you." But. as I began to talk with her, a deep sense of compassion came over me and I felt blanketed in peace.

After we talked, I excused myself and went back to the car to gather what I could find in the line of food. I talked for a second with Craig, telling him her need and he pulled out his wallet and handed me a bill that seemed generous but appropriate for us to give.

I took my bag of fruit in one hand and the folded bill in the other. She took the fruit and was so grateful. Then I said, "May I pray for you?" Her response was enthusiastically, "Oh yes!"

I touched her hand with mine and began to pray. I don't remember what I said but I do remember I was praying things I normally wouldn't have thought to pray. I literally felt like the Holy Spirit was praying through me.

When I finished, I handed her the money and when she looked at it, she seemed shocked. Immediately she expressed her heartfelt gratefulness.

I was so thankful I had listened to His still small voice and had not walked away.

Rest Stop

In a situation like this, I always check with God first. I can trust Him to show me if I am to *partner* with Him to help with an assignment.

> "Never let your brotherly love fail, nor refuse to extend your hospitality to strangers—sometimes men have entertained angels unawares."
>
> Hebrews 13:2 Phillips

WILL WE SURVIVE?

Remain in His Presence and keep your eyes fixed on Jesus.

Our Alaska Airline flight from Seattle to Palm Springs was both horribly intense and unexpectedly precious! However, I hope to never experience a situation like it again.

Miles from our destination, we were being tossed, jerked and free-falling, due to unexpectedly high (70+ mph) winds. People were gasping, screaming, swearing, and loudly expressing how fearful they were.

I was grateful to have Craig next to me, and firmly held on to his arm as I prayed in my thoughts, *Lord, I don't know if this is our time to step into eternity, but I'm ready to meet You if it is. I just ask that You calm down the passengers on this flight and use this terrifying experience to speak to their hearts. Draw them to Yourself and help them realize that YOU are all they need, to let go of the fear.*

As I prayed, we continued to be jerked back and forth with everyone wondering if we would survive the flight. I heard a lady in the seat behind us say, "I have flown all over the world and have never had an experience like this!" She continued, "Are we all going to die?" That comment didn't help those around her who were dealing with such intense fear.

Immediately, my thoughts turned to the man sitting in the window seat next to me. We had not spoken. He had been sleeping, until the jarring and tossing began, but awoke and looked absolutely startled. I said, "Don't be afraid, we're going to be fine." He then expressed his own fear and said, "I'm not so sure we are. I've never experienced anything this severe."

I thought, *if we do crash, I may only have moments left to make certain he is ready to meet Jesus.* I said, "May I ask your name? Mine is Karen." He didn't seem anxious to exchange pleasantries, but he said his name was Steve. I used it as often as possible when I spoke to him, to help keep him centered in his thoughts.

"Steve, you don't know me but the fact that we are going through such horrible turbulence, I sense you are feeling very fearful. May I ask you the most important question you will ever be asked?" He hesitantly answered, "Sure, go ahead." I continued, "I really don't believe we will crash because I have complete peace. However, I think it's important that we are ready in any situation to know the answer to this question: *Do you know where you will spend eternity when you take your last breath?*"

Immediately, he said, "Yes, I know."

I waited for an explanation because I hoped he wouldn't say, "I've tried to live a good life." Instead, he said. "I have invited Jesus Christ into my heart and life, and I know I will go to heaven."

I told him I was grateful to hear his response and I was still certain that everything was going to be fine. *We just needed to keep focused on Jesus* and pray for our pilot.

As I continued to observe his fears and lack of trust that God would take care of us, I wondered if he was like so many Christians who asked Jesus into their heart, to be assured of getting their spiritual fire insurance, to escape hell, but there was no real relationship and trust in Jesus.

With all the commotion, it was impossible to carry a conversation with him or I would have loved to encourage him to take one further step with Jesus and ask Him to be *Lord* of his life. That would mean asking God to be in control. At this point, he was obviously trying to control his own circumstances, but the fear and swearing were only escalating.

As we arrived near the airport, the pilot tried landing in the opposite direction, as he had been instructed by the tower. The winds were so intense, the landing had to be aborted when we were about 15ft. from the ground. I was concerned our plane would flip over but the pilot kept all the crazy gyrations under control. He pulled up once again and headed west, towards the Ontario Airport, a 20-minute flight away. There was a relief among the passengers, thinking we had escaped the winds. It simply wasn't true!

When the passengers realized we hadn't left the winds behind, the fears returned. I wasn't afraid but my heartbeat had definitely increased, due to stress. I so wished I could stand up and use the intercom. There were things that could be said to help the passengers take their focus off of fear, in an attempt to calm them down.

When the airplane landed at Ontario Airport, the pilot gave the passengers a choice to leave the plane and find a car rental to return to Palm Springs, or to stay on the plane until the Palm Springs Airport gave us the clearance to return. I was certain the control tower would know when it was safe to return.

Steve stood up immediately, saying, "I'm getting the heck out of here!" He crawled over me and took off with more than half of the passengers.

When people are really fearful, their emotions can quickly turn to anger. That anger can then be passed on to others, especially when there is a crowd with their own personal ideas of how things should have been handled. They weren't willing to accept that the pilots had done everything possible with our plane and even the best of pilots couldn't have done anything more. The winds were just too severe.

After the large crowd of passengers left, others gradually trickled out of the exit door, knowing they would not be allowed to return to the cabin. The doors were locked behind them.

The flight staff wasn't helpful because they were also feeling fearful and stressed. They made no attempt at making any comments over the loudspeaker, to calm down the remaining passengers; they were waiting to receive the go-ahead to return to the Palm Springs Airport. The silence on their part gave opportunity for the passengers to talk between themselves, with conversations becoming more negative by the minute.

Someone needed to help! I walked up to the front of the plane to talk with the flight attendants. I asked what information had they been given and asked if they could share it with the passengers. They stood there with a blank look, having no clue as to what they could do. I suggested they come up with something creative to say over the intercom, because anger and blame were escalating among the passengers in the back of the cabin.

Finally, the flight hostess got on the intercom and did her best but it wasn't good enough. More passengers asked to leave the plane. I thought, a *Kindergartener could have done a better job at calming everyone*. (I know, that wasn't a kind thought but it was true). So, I began to pray for the pilots and flight hostesses.

After 1½ hours of waiting on the plane, the pilot decided to *try* again. Within moments, our plane took off, to return to Palm Springs. We all assumed the pilot wouldn't have returned unless the winds had calmed and it was safe to fly. Unfortunately, the turbulence was still severe. It was only a 20min. flight but it seemed forever.

Then, something amazing happened to me. I felt the Lord guiding my thoughts and showing me how I could position my body in a protective manner. I was to take hold of both sides of the back of the seat in front of me and brace my feet wide apart to keep my body from falling from side to side. (We learned this when we leased a yacht in the San Juan Islands of Washington state and had to cross high swells of water). That helped my body to be more stable in facing the effects of the winds that were jerking our 737 jet from side to side and up and down.

People's voices became louder than before, as they expressed their fears with more screaming and swearing. As I sat in my awkward stance, with my seat-belt tightened around me, the Lord gave me the next thought: to bow my head so that the top of my head was braced firmly into the back of the seat in front of me.

A Bible story of the fearful disciples on the boat with Jesus, who was sound asleep, came to mind. I thought, *if Jesus could calm the storm and bring peace on their little fishing boat, He can bring calm to my soul, which is my mind, emotions and will.*

I began to quietly pray and thank God for His protection over our plane. Within seconds, I felt a stillness and peace as I continued to sit in my awkward position with my eyes closed, and the top of my head, still leaning into the seat in front of me.

I made a conscious choice to get in His Presence.

The plane was still jerking and dipping but Jesus was in it with me. It felt like only He and I were in that plane! Yes, I still had to hold on to the sides of the seat in front of me, with my head pressed into that seat, but the calm, quietness and peace in my spirit drowned out the loud noise by other passengers. An old hymn came to mind: *It Is Well With My Soul.*

I began to softly sing, *"When peace like a river attendeth my way.... When sorrows like sea billows roll.....Whatever my lot, thou hast taught me to say...It is well, it is well with my soul."*

Oh, so softly I talked to Jesus and worshiped His sweet Presence. It was beyond precious and I was wishing I could help other passengers discover the peace I was experiencing.

Finally, the plane came to a rough landing, and a loud applause exploded. These were the same passengers who had been cursing the pilot earlier. They finally realized we had actually landed safely and were still alive. All I could say was, "Lord, you are so faithful," as I let go of the grip on the seat, lifted my head, and sat up straight.

We were seated towards the back of the plane so we waited for a few minutes to let the fearful passengers rush off the plane.

Across from us and one row back, in a window seat, a 5-year-old boy, with his mother, had remained very quiet during all the noise and wild gyrations of the plane. When they stood up to finally leave, an older lady, across the aisle from my husband's seat, put her arm out to stop the child who was leaving. She looked him in his eyes and said, "Young man, weren't you afraid when the plane was jerking all around?"

Those of us, in hearing distance, were surprised by his response, "Oh no! That was fun! It *was* like the rides at Disneyland!" Then, he went on his way as though he was a seasoned traveler.

We need to be more like that young, trusting child. He was taking a fun ride and didn't expect anything bad to happen.

When it was our turn to leave, we walked down the long aisle to the front of the cabin. The pilot and flight hostesses were standing at the exit. I looked into the eyes of the pilot, smiled at him and said, "I'm certain God guided your hands as you landed this plane. I was praying for you." He looked shocked and grateful to hear kind words, after the negative responses he had received from others.

I'm grateful for the precious lesson for which God taught me: The key to any tragic, difficult, or painful trial is to…

Remain in His Presence and keep your eyes fixed on Jesus, not on circumstances.

I knew I had heard this over 35 years before, when I asked my 89-yr-old mother what advice she would like to leave each of her six children. Her health was failing quickly and she was only weeks away from passing. She said:

KEEP YOUR EYES FIXED ON JESUS!

Those six words say it all! And, those are the exact words I want to leave with my family, before I slip into eternity.

I LOVE YOU

*I was convinced old hurts could
be erased by those three words.*

My father was 50 years old when I was born. As I grew up, I knew he and my mother loved me, but I never remember either of them saying those words to me or to any of my five older siblings.

When my dad turned 89, he had a heart attack that landed him in the hospital. Days later, when mother went to pick him up to drive him home, she went into his room as he changed from his hospital gown to street clothes.

Suddenly, she cried out, "Joseph, why is there blood on your hospital gown?!"

That discovery changed the whole trajectory of my father's life. He was diagnosed with bladder cancer and eventually, the decision was made not to have chemo or surgery.

He made that decision because he knew he had lived a long, full life and chose not to go through the effects of chemo. His choice was to allow God to take him home to heaven, whenever that amazing moment would take place.

I was 39, married, and had one son. And, I had no idea that I would have a precious Divine Appointment with my own father. It happened within two weeks before he stepped into eternity.

I drove from our home in Seattle and headed 60 miles north where my parents lived. I had made this trip many times but I felt this visit was going to be special.

We had no idea how much time dad had left, so I sought out every opportunity to be with him. On my visits, I stayed with mother each evening to make certain she was adjusting to the possibility of the imminent passing of her husband.

One day when I was alone with dad, an idea came to me that I had never given thought to before. I stood next to the side of his hospital bed and began to gently speak to him.

"Dad, did your parents ever tell you that they loved you?" There was a long pause before he responded. I knew he was searching back in his memory bank to try to remember the years of his childhood. However, he looked down and gently, and oh so slowly said, "I guess I can't remember that far back but I don't think they ever did."

Now I knew it was time to ask, "Dad, do you ever remember telling any of your children that you love them?" Another pause, but he knew the answer. His eyes began to water. "They all knew that I loved them, didn't they?"

Then, God put an idea in my mind and I was anxious to see what could happen. I prepared my thoughts and my spirit to ask a very direct question. I was convinced it could begin something amazing for our entire family.

I said, "Dad, would you like to begin with me and tell me that you love me?"

It was so foreign to him, like it is for those of that generation in which he was raised. Tears began to fall and you would think I was trying to *teach him* a new language. I guess I was – a love language.

I took it very slowly. I knew all kinds of things were running through his thoughts: his mortality, wanting his children to know he loved them, even though they were 39 through 61 years of age.

I brought back the focus on those three simple words. "Dad, can you look at me and say, "I love you"? He calmed down his emotions but each time he would start to speak, he would break and begin to cry. I got closer to him and took his hand and said, "*Dad, I love you.*" Without hesitation, he responded, "Oh honey, I love you too." Then, he really cried.

The emotional dam had broken, and he wanted to say it over and over! We cried and laughed together, and I said,

"Okay dad, would you like to say it to your other five children?" I told him that I wanted each child to remember the day when he told them he loved them. He understood.

When the oldest brother, Henry, came for a visit later that day, I stayed quiet as they chatted for a few moments. When there was a lull in the conversation, I gently said, "Dad, was there something you wanted to tell Henry?" He started out, "Henry, you know how we've worked together all these years and often got frustrated with each other? Well, there's something I want you to know. The tears came again, but we waited. Then he said, "I want you to know that I love you." My brother waited a moment and gently responded, "I love you too, dad."

I saw a new freedom in my father's countenance and he was ready to share it with all those he loved.

After that breakthrough, he wanted me to call the other four siblings who lived quite a distance away. He wanted to talk to them on the phone and say those three amazing words. I started making the calls and he followed through with each of his children. The result was amazing!

When he finished, his heart was so full of love that when his family visited, he never forgot to tell each one that he loved them.

The day of dad's memorial, as my siblings and mother were riding in the black limousine to the gravesite, my sister, 6 years older than I, turned to me and said, "Karen, do you know what I remember most about dad?" There were a number of stories she could have shared, but she said, "I vividly remember the day when Dad called me. He was in the hospital and told me that he loved me." In my thoughts *I said, thank you Lord for replacing old memories with this special one.*

I never dreamed this Divine Appointment, with my own father, would turn out to be so amazing. This was not an isolated struggle. I have learned there are many families, even today, who find it difficult to be real with their emotions.

Many years later, before my step-father-in-law passed, I had the same experience again. He had only one living birth child when he died at 94. One day, as we were talking about his wishes for a memorial, I brought up the same question I had asked my own father.

I was surprised how he was more than interested to talk about this subject.

After asking him if he had ever told his daughter those 3 important words, he wanted me to understand that he loved her and appreciated how she cared for his every need. He couldn't remember if he had ever told her he loved her. He was certain, however, that she knew he did. Then, after he gave it more thought he said, "What do I say to make sure she knows?" I shared how it takes only 3 simple words.

Then, I had him practice by saying them to me, so that he would be more comfortable in using these words with her. With an excitement in his countenance, he decided the next time he saw her, he wanted to be certain to tell her.

We had been visiting him at his assisted living apartment for a few days, but would be leaving early the next morning to return to southern California. That evening we said our goodbyes and walked across the street to our motel.

Little did I know that he was concerned that he might forget his plan, due to his failing memory. So, he wrote a note to remind himself what he wanted to share with his daughter. He placed the little paper on the small table next to his recliner.

The next morning, after he returned from breakfast at the dining hall, he sat in his recliner and looked over the newspaper. Suddenly, he saw the note on the side table. He was delighted he had left the note by his chair, to be reminded that she would be coming that morning. He was determined not to forget what he had planned.

Within moments, he heard the door open and immediately, without saying *good morning*, he blurted out, "Mara Marie, I have something I have to tell you!"

She sensed the urgency in his voice but responded, "Dad, can it wait long enough for me to take off my coat?" He chuckled as he realized his anxiousness.

After she had unloaded things from her hands and hung up her coat, she walked over to him and said, "Now what would you like to tell me?"

With deep seriousness, he said, "Mara, you know that I love you, don't you?" She responded, "Well, of course I do." He continued, "But, I don't think I ever told you that I love you… but I do."

She had never heard those words from her father in the 68 years of her life and they brought joy to her heart. She had always known that his generation was known for holding in their emotions and not talking about love. That day, the generational deficiency had been broken.

Some months later, her dad passed away. He had always been a good dad, but her relationship with him grew deeper as she took care of him towards the end of his life. She was left with precious memories, and the highlight was her dad telling her that he loved her.

No matter how old a person is, those 3 simple words, *I Love You*, can heal wounds of past memories and create an atmosphere for healthy relationships.

SURE WASN'T MY PLAN

God's plan had literally redirected
my plans and my steps.

God simply amazes me how He gets my attention! When a Divine Appointment happens, it's because HE sets it up. Then, He works in me without me even realizing it.

I found a scripture from Ezekiel 37:1 (NLT) which says, *"The Lord took hold of me, and I was carried away by the Spirit of the Lord..."* I related to this verse because after this experience, I felt His plan had literally redirected my plan and my steps.

Yes, I know the application of this verse is out of context in which it was originally intended, however, that's how it felt when I finally realized where I ended up. Let me explain.

One Sunday morning, while visiting out-of-state friends, we went with them to visit their new church. I had no plans to get involved in conversation with any stranger. I had come to worship and be encouraged by the message of their amazing pastor.

I should have known from past experience that His plans are on His schedule, not mine. When He has an assignment for me, I may not feel like being bothered, but He waits until I surrender my will.

After years of training in this area, my heart's desire is to be available to *partner* with Him, to accomplish what He has planned.

After worship, an associate pastor announced, "Please take a moment to greet someone this morning and help them feel welcome, before you sit down."

I was dealing with a painful hip so I just sat down. Besides I didn't feel led to meet anyone new.

Suddenly, I noticed a young man sitting 3 rows in front of us. He turned around and walked directly back to my husband and firmly shook his hand. Then, I thought, *I know I've seen that guy before.* As I searched my mind, I could not come up with a time or place I would have met him. It was a most unusual sensation and the thought kept returning throughout the service.

Even though my mind had been distracted by that thought, I had no plans to go over to him after the service and introduce myself. My plan was to quietly walk out with my husband and our hosts. We had plans to go to a nearby restaurant for brunch, and I was hungry!

I shouldn't have been surprised that God might have a different plan!

The sermon ended and we stood for the closing prayer. As we exited our row, our hosts and my husband, in front of me, came to the end of the row and turned left. I turned right.

What was I doing?

Before I realized what was happening, I walked over to the familiar looking stranger, telling him that he had a very familiar face and I wondered how I might know him.

We introduced ourselves and exchanged conversation, but couldn't come up with an answer. So, I smiled and excused myself.

As I turned around to walk towards the back of the church, I noticed the man was close by my side. I unexpectedly said, "Do you have any children?"

Why in the world would I have asked that question? It was none of my business. Then, I was shocked when he responded. I realized the *real* conversation that God had planned, had just begun.

"I have two children and neither of them want a relationship with me. My daughter is 18 and my son is 23."

He went on to share how he told them how they needed to get their lives together and follow Jesus. As I stopped to listen, it all sounded like a lecture that his kids had probably heard over and over. I sensed he may be divorced and his time with them was limited.

He continued to share all the things that were wrong with his son and daughter. I realized he was deeply concerned but God showed me the bigger picture. I couldn't hold back any longer. "Bo," I said, "How is your method of lecturing to your children working for you?"

Surprised by my question, he stood for a moment, deep in thought and looking to the floor. He quietly responded, "Well, I guess it isn't."

I continued, "Would you be willing to try something different?" He raised his head and enthusiastically said, "YES, I would!"

I explained how the years of training his children were over, now that they were young adults. I continued, "Now, God wants you to spend time in prayer for them. Actually, your assignment will be to pray for them daily, the rest of your life.

As a matter of fact, every time you start to worry about their wrong choices, you need to consciously STOP! Then, ask the Holy Spirit to draw them to Himself and give them a hunger to have a personal relationship with Him." I explained how adult children usually think they have all the answers and don't want to hear their parent's lectures. "But they do want to *see* our love."

This was a new concept to him and he listened intently. I suggested that every time he saw his daughter and son, to ask the Lord to give him specific and positive words of affirmation (with no preaching), and to show love, love, and more love in the same way the Lord shows us love when we are going our own way, doing our own thing, and not listening to Him.

A new countenance came over his face. Slowly, with impact, he said, "YOU ARE THE ANSWER TO MY PRAYERS! I recently asked the Lord what I could do to change my kid's behavior and their response to me. You just gave me the answer!"

Gently, I said, "Bo, you can't change them. All God asks you to do is pray for them, love them, and bless them. When they see Jesus in you, they will be drawn to Him, and you, too."

The thoughts kept coming and I kept visualizing what God could do in the relationships with this man's children. I continued, "Another thought to consider is to ask each of them, separately, what they feel you can do to be a better dad. However, if they give you an answer, be sure not to get defensive, disagreeable or negative. Just thank them for their honesty. I bet they'll be shocked by your Godly response.

I knew I needed to warn him, so I continued. "Don't be surprised if the enemy brings you to a place where you think...*After everything I've done for my kids, how can they treat me this way?* Don't allow Satan to bring in wrong expectations that can lead to disappointment or depression. *Just start praising the Lord for what He is going to do in them, and in you also."*

I encouraged him to ask the Lord to open his heart of understanding and show him what *He* wants to do in *his* heart and life; to make him the father He wants him to be to his young adult children.

Suddenly, I realized my husband and hosts had walked over to the restaurant, nearby, so I felt I needed to excuse myself and catch-up with them. However, it appeared Bo still had something on his heart that needed to be said. He emphasized, "This has been a Divine Appointment! Yes! This *has* been a *real* Divine Appointment!"

I smiled because he had no idea how divine appointments happen to me all the time. It was a joy that he recognized it even before I did.

Then he ended with, "Thank you for allowing the Lord to use you by answering my prayer."

I asked the Lord to bless him and his children. Then I walked away thinking, "Did the Lord just give me a strong sense that I recognized this young man, but in reality, we had never met.?"

I felt like I had been 'set up' by God, once again!

If he hadn't put that thought strongly in my mind that I recognized him from somewhere, I would have totally missed this Divine Appointment.

It wasn't my plan, but it certainly was a good one. The Lord had physically turned me in Bo's direction and opened my mouth to speak His words.

As I walked away, I whispered to the Lord, *thank you Lord for your faithfulness in answering Bo's request. And, once again, allowing me to partner with You to accomplish what You had already planned.*

I'M EVERYWHERE

I didn't want to get involved because
these things can take a lot my time.

t was Thanksgiving and our son and family had flown down from Seattle, leaving the rain for the sunny California desert.

On their last morning with us, I dropped them off at the edge of the San Jacinto mountains where they started their two-hour hike up the steep trail. I had errands to run and my first stop was the library, returning books I had checked-out for our grandsons.

When I arrived at the library, I noticed an elderly lady standing at the back of her car with the trunk open.

A thought passed through my mind; *she looks like she's going to need help.* She had a walker, bag of heavy books and what looked to be an equally heavy purse. I thought, *how is she going to handle all of that weight with her stooped-over frail looking frame of a body.*

Sadly, a second thought rushed into my mind, *I don't want to get involved because these things can take a lot of time.*

I've had enough experience with these kinds of situations to know that it wouldn't be a matter of just helping her carry in books; it would mean *talking* and *more* talking.

I took a deep breath. I knew what my Lord would want me to do, so, I turned and walked towards her and asked, "Could I help you with some of those items? They look heavy."

She stood a little taller and smiled as she answered, "Oh, I'd be so grateful for your help."

We slowly walked towards the short distance to the library door, with her stopping to talk along the way, in addition to her telling me her name was Alice.

I tried to be interested in her conversation about her family, who lived out of town and the fact that she was 94 and all alone.

But, I needed to hurry so I could get all my projects finished before I had to pick up my family at the base of the hiking trail. I wanted to savor every minute with them before it was time for them to catch their return flight home.

Alice and I eventually made it to the desk where I scanned each book to be returned. It was obvious she was not finished talking, and when I asked if she had anyone to assist her at home, she mentioned how her children wanted her to move into a retirement facility. But she made it clear, "I'm independent and I don't want to move out of my home!" Yes, she needed help…but on *her* terms.

Before I left, I gave her my phone number and told her to feel free to call if she needed help with anything. I knew the Lord had brought her into my life, just like all the Divine Appointments He had brought.

As I drove away from the library, I got specific with the Lord and audibly spoke with Him. "Lord, I know you keep bringing these people into my life, but how am I going to keep up, especially with those who are so needy for follow-up?"

I took a deep breath and blew out my stress. I tried to figure out what He had in mind. Once again, I said, "Help me understand Lord!"

I really didn't expect an answer. It's kind of like when I've been frustrated in a situation and I share it with my husband. I'm merely venting and I don't need him to fix it. I just need him to listen.

> *I wondered if God was really listening or if He just expected me to trust Him.*

When the answer came, it wasn't what I expected! Usually, He gives me an impression deep down in my spirit. Then I say, "Lord, was that really You?"

No, this time the words He spoke were so clear, it was as though He was sitting right next to me in the car!

I heard him audibly say, *I'M EVERYWHERE*.

I was so shocked, I turned to my right to see who was sitting next to me! My heart was racing! I didn't even question how it was possible but *I knew I heard His voice*!

My spirit knew it was Him. I clearly understood what He was saying to me and the tears began to well up in my eyes. I couldn't continue driving in my emotional state of mind, so I pulled over to the side of the road.

My mind was full of thoughts regarding the many past Divine Appointments He had given me over the years. I had always felt such joy after one took place. And I would often spend time standing in awe and praising Him.

But this experience went *beyond* all of those. Now, I understood more clearly than ever before… *they had all been HIM!*

Later, a scripture came to mind, "…whatever you did for one of the least of these… you did it for me." (Matthew 25:40 NIV).

It finally made perfect sense to me. Even though the Lord had allowed all these different ones to come into my life, my response was the most important thing. I could choose to ignore them and walk away, or, I could respond with love towards them, as though I were *ministering to Him.*

Believe me, there were many times I turned away and ignored His leading. Although, I lost the most amazing opportunity to minister love to others, and to Him.

According to scripture (Matthew 25:35-36), if God tells me to go and feed a person, give water or clothe someone, to visit a sick person or someone in prison...I want to be committed to DO IT!

If He has directed me to do these things,
it will be as though I have done it for Him.

Years ago, I used to help these people, until I learned what most of them were doing with the money they received.

Now, I ask the Lord to show me what the *real* need is. Sometimes I give a protein bar or bottled water I have in the car. Then there are times when I know I am to give them money. Each situation is *different.*

All I know is that Jesus requests my personal involvement in caring for others' personal needs.

Do you have any idea how exciting it is to be part of something the Lord plans for you to do?

Days later, I was listening to Bridget, my *next* Divine Appointment. She talked on and on, and I thought about what God had said to me…"I'm everywhere." Suddenly, she looked different to me, because of a completely different paradigm…

I was ministering love to
Him by listening to her!

I knew I was in His presence because I was filled with unspeakable JOY!

Oh my…after all these years of ministering to strangers, how did I miss this amazing truth?

It became very clear after He audibly spoke to me with such clarity. I will never forget His poignant words:

I'm everywhere.

FAITHFUL TO THE END

Such selfless and amazing love.

A few months before my 89-year-old mother passed away, I observed a situation I hope to never forget. If I am ever in an experience like it, I trust I will apply the precious lesson I learned through it. Let me explain:

My mother had walked with the Lord for over 75 years. She had been a chaplain in prison, ministered in nursing homes, spoke at a number of Christian Women's groups, and had no fear of talking with or helping strangers wherever she saw a need.

During her life, she brought several needy souls to the saving knowledge of Jesus Christ and was dearly loved by those she had mentored. I was certain God would continue to use her to be a blessing to the end of her life.

Mother *deeply* loved the Lord and was a mighty prayer warrior. However, as her health deteriorated, so did her cognitive abilities; her memory, judgment, and reasoning declined. Sadly, she became more self-centered, negative, and demanding.

I was the youngest of 6 children and ended up being her advocate and caregiver the last year of her life. However, when she came to a place where she needed round-the-clock nursing care, I had to make the difficult decision to have her placed in a nursing care facility.

She had definite expectations that I, personally, would take care of her, but after accessing the whole situation, it wasn't possible.

I had chosen the best nursing facility in the area. However, because there were no private rooms, things got really difficult when a roommate was moved into her room the second day after she arrived.

After meeting the roommate and talking with her daughter, I thought, *Praise God, the new roommate is a precious Christian woman.* She was in her late 90s and I was thrilled because I felt she was a perfect match for mother. I hoped they'd be able to share their love of Jesus and have wonderful fellowship together.

However, on their 5th day as roommates, my hopes were dashed. I heard mother complain to the head nurse, firmly saying, "I want you to get that woman out of my room! I don't like her!"

I was shocked at mom's request. I was even *more* shocked when the head-nurse honored her request and moved this sweet woman to a different room down the hall. Mother thought she owned the room and did ***not*** want anyone moving into her space!

After a couple days of solitude, a different roommate was wheeled into the room. This one turned out to be a serious challenge!

Once again, mother didn't like her either. Actually, the entire nursing staff struggled with this woman's angry disposition. She swore at everyone, was loud, angry, and made it clear that she wanted to return to her own home.

I so hoped my mother would see this angry soul as a project because she clearly needed Jesus, and mom had lots of experience handling difficult people.

But, only a short time later, the head nurse realized this was a really poor match and moved roommate #2 to a different room, at my mother's request.

I continued to visit with mother on a daily basis, trying to do everything I could to encourage her and help her to adjust. Nothing helped. All it did was exhaust me and my own health started to deteriorate.

During this time, I often talked to mom's first roommate's family, as we passed in the hallway. They always spoke lovingly of their precious Christian mother. She was the most gentle, soft-spoken and loving soul I had ever met. No matter how difficult her circumstances, she wanted to honor the Lord in her life. And, in time, I learned that roommate #2, mother's cantankerous roommate, had been moved into several different rooms, but no one wanted her until they moved her into mom's roommate #1, the gentle and sweet Christian elderly woman.

I was anxious to see what God was going to do and often prayed for this cranky roommate #2.

In a short time, mother was given a third roommate. This woman didn't talk and kept to herself. Of course, mom didn't accept her either; however, this time the head nurse refused to remove the roommate and mother had to accept her.

A few weeks later, I learned that the sweet Christian elderly woman, mother's 1st roommate, went home to be with Jesus. When her daughter came to pick up her mother's belongings, I told her how much I had enjoyed her sweet mother and how sorry I was that my mom had been so unkind to her.

The daughter said, "Well, God had a purpose in mind when He allowed the surly roommate to be placed in my mother's room. Did you know my mother led that woman to Christ, the day before she died? There was such a change in that mean woman's life I could hardly believe she was the same person!" Then, with great enthusiasm, the daughter continued, "Did you also hear that the next day, it was only a few hours after my mother's death that her roommate also was ushered into eternity with our Lord?"

I wanted to cry and shout *halleluiah* all at the same time. My heart was filled with joy because of what the Lord had done! That precious Christian woman had been faithful to her Lord even in the last days of her earthly life. She had led that difficult woman to ask Jesus into her heart and life, and then they both were ushered into eternity within the same day! Only our gracious Lord could have orchestrated it.

This isn't the end of the story. During all my visits to the nursing home, I had also met the granddaughter of the *challenging* roommate – #2. I was delighted to learn of the granddaughter's relationship with Jesus! She had been praying faithfully for years that her grandmother would surrender to the Lord before she died.

One Sunday evening, my husband, son and I stopped at a Dairy Queen for a quick dessert. Before we had finished, this *same* granddaughter walked into the restaurant with her small family.

Her grandmother had passed a couple weeks earlier and she recognized me as she entered the restaurant. I stood up and walked over to greet her and looked into her eyes and said, "Aren't you thrilled what God did with your grandmother?"

The young woman looked at me with a puzzled and wrinkled brow look. She said, "What are you talking about? The last time I saw her, about 3 days before she died, she still wanted nothing to do with Jesus. I could hardly handle the pain of fearing she would slip into eternity without knowing my precious Jesus."

As she spoke, I was shaking my head back and forth and quickly interrupted with, "No, no, no!

Didn't you know that her sweet Christian roommate led her to Jesus the day before she died? And that's not all. The next day, the Christian roommate passed away in the morning and your grandmother followed her that afternoon?"

The young woman broke into tears of joy and said, "I never knew! I never knew! I thought she died without knowing Christ!"

I assured her that God had answered her prayers and she would someday see her grandmother in heaven.

Wow! Even though this story took place 35 years ago, it has made a deep and lasting impression on my heart.

I still get emotional when I think about it. Matter-of-fact, I asked the Lord to help me be like my mother's 1st roommate who had put other's needs before herself, had shown His amazing love to her crabby roommate, and then led her to Jesus. Her love for this angry roommate was one of wanting the latter to be forgiven of her sins, so that when she died, she would spend eternity with Jesus.

I thought: *This is such selfless and amazing love. She had been faithful to the end.*

What did I learn from this experience?

First, I learned how the brain can change as we get old and hopefully our children will still respond in love to us, even if we get cranky and our personality changes.

Also, If I end up in a nursing care facility, I pray God will also give me an opportunity to lead one more lost soul to Jesus before I die. I've asked Him to give me *His* amazing grace, to remain… FAITHFUL TO THE END.

BEAUTIFUL LILLIA

In the blink of an eye, she stepped into eternity.

When I learned the news of Lillia's tragic car accident, the shock settled in and I honestly didn't think it was possible. She had *just* turned 17.

I first met Lillia at the wedding of our son and daughter-in-law, Gregory and Christy, held in Washington D.C.

Lillia was Christy's darling niece and flower girl. I didn't get to see her again because her family lived in Florida and we lived in Washington state. However, I followed her life through updates from Christy.

On the afternoon of April 24, 2018, I received the fateful call from Christy. She told me she had received a call from her mother but couldn't make sense of what she was trying to say. In the shock of the moment, all Christy could understand through the sobbing words of her mother were: "Accident…Died … Lillia."

It just didn't make sense! As we pieced the words together, it became something we could only hope was *not* true!

In time, we learned the truth. Lillia had left early from school that day. She drove to her grandmother's home for lunch and then headed to her part-time job at Trinity Spine, in the physical therapy department. She had never once been late for work so when she didn't show up that day, the office called her mother. They had also seen a 3-car accident in front of their building, but didn't realize she was part of it.

Soon, it went on-line with the Tampa Florida News. The pictures of the charcoal gray car, crushed between two other vehicles, was clearly Lillia's car. Yet, we still weren't certain she was actually deceased. The news focused on the man who ran from the accident. Then, later it was discovered that this man was a friend of the driver, who jumped from the passenger seat of the old SUV, and ran with the back-pack full of drugs. He was found 4-hours later.

The driver, who had blown through the stop light, as Lillia was turning, hit her car and killed her *instantly*. After his vehicle came to a stop, he realized his leg had been broken, and he tried to climb into the passenger seat to make it look like he was not the driver. But because his DNA remained on the driver's side airbag, it proved he was guilty. The 3rd man in the back seat, had been trying to urge the driver to get off the road because of his erratic driving, but the driver wouldn't listen.

Forensics discovered the driver had ridiculous amounts of crystal meth in his system and it was confirmed by the full backpack of drugs his buddy in crime was carrying. When the guy was found, he cooperated and admitted they were shooting up drugs the night before and the day of the accident.

From the first moment I learned about the accident, I sensed God's call to intercede in prayer, on behalf of her family. The shock would be tremendous throughout the entire community *and* with her many high school friends. Most of all, I knew her family needed to be covered by God's grace, to walk through such a tragic experience.

As I began to pray, I couldn't understand my own brokenness, the uncontrolled tears and pain in my chest as though I had personally lost a child or grandchild of my own. For two days, the grieving would come and I soon realized it was God's call to keep me praying again and again.

The third day was the *graveside service* and m*emorial.* The Lord awakened me at 4 a.m. and I went straight to our guest room where I could be alone to pray. Lillia's family was my deepest concern and focus for prayer.

Our son and family had flown from Washington state to Florida, to be with Christy's family. I was grateful they could all be together, but after the hours of weeping and praying, I felt a deep connection and longed to be with them.

I cancelled plans that morning, knowing the Lord was asking me to be in fervent prayer during the two services. I was alone and began to simply pray for HIS *Peace,* HIS *Grace,* and HIS *Strength* for the family, as they walked through this difficult day of saying goodbye to Lillia.

Then it happened again! The uncontrolled weeping flooded over me and I sobbed out the words to my precious Lord, "Why can't I be there with them?" In my spirit, I heard Him say... *You need to be here so you can focus on praying and to be My messenger*!

In time, the grieving stopped and my praying fell silent.

My eyes were closed and I had the most beautiful VISION from Heaven. *I saw Jesus* in his long white stately linen robe, standing near the edge of heaven and gently blowing His presence over those who were attending the graveside service. I didn't see His face but I knew it was His hands cupped around each side of His mouth. I could hear Him take a slow, deep, full breath and then, ever so gently and slowly, blow it out through his pursed lips.

The graveside service was taking place about 1-½ hours before the memorial. In my experience, this service is usually a very emotional time; it is the *letting go* of the loved one. It would seem so final and those in attendance needed to feel the calming Presence of the Lord Jesus, as He blew the gentle *BREATH of HIS SPIRIT* down upon those in attendance, like a cool morning mist that brought comfort and peace.

Then, with my eyes still closed, *I saw Lillia.* She was standing about 3 feet to the right of Jesus and was tenderly scooping something up with her arms and hands, that were held in a circular position, the size of a large exercise ball, but it was light like a feather. Over and over again she would continue scooping and gently tossing it in the air, over the edge of heaven. She somehow knew she was covering those at her graveside.

In the vision, I asked the Lord what Lillia was doing. He spoke into my spirit, telling me she was throwing *BLESSINGS.* She had the biggest radiant smile on her face and looked almost giddy, as she received such joy in sharing God's blessings from heaven with those she loved.

When Lillia finished, she was drawn to turn and face the glowing heavenly light behind where the Lord had been standing. She rejoiced because she knew she was in His Presence. As she raised her hands high in worship, it was clear to me that her spirit felt at home; she was now with her precious Jesus!

The vision ended. How I longed for it to continue. All I could do was cry tears of JOY!

After I finished writing this story, I decided to contact Lillia's mother and ask if she knew the meaning of her daughter's first and middle names. She enthusiastically but gently responded, "Oh yes, the meanings are, *PURE GRACE.*"

I thought, *no wonder Lillia was so precious. Even the meaning of her names was demonstrated in her sweet demeanor.*

Then her mother graciously ended with, "And, she was *pure grace* starting in the womb." When I heard that last phrase, my eyes watered as I sensed the depth of this mother's love.

Thankfully, their separation is only for a short time because someday, she, too, will step into eternity and they will be together again.

HE TOOK OVER

*Trusting Him brings us to a place of
complete peace because He's in control.*

et me start by saying, I believe in prayer and I
believe in healing. Personally, I have been
miraculously healed at least *five times* and probably
even more. So, I know that God does heal. However, in
the past, I struggled in believing that others could be
healed when I prayed for them.

Each Sunday morning our pastor announces that if anyone
would like to come to the front with any need and receive
prayer – the pastors and elders would be available to pray
at the end of the service.

A few years ago, my husband and I had been asked to be
elders. We were thrilled to volunteer to be greeters and
welcome people as they entered the sanctuary each
Sunday, but I felt uncomfortable taking on other positions.

Then, one Sunday, I was shocked when our Pastor Fred
asked if my husband and I would be willing to go to the
front, after the service, and be available to pray.

After he walked away, I firmly grabbed my husband's
hand and pulled his tall body to me so I could whisper in

his ear, "There is NO way I am going up there to pray for people. I would make a fool out of myself." Craig looked at me with raised eye brows and whispered, "We will be fine and we'll do what the pastor has asked of us."

Of course, when the service ended, Craig took my hand and started out into the aisle, expecting me to follow. I pulled back and said, "I don't feel comfortable doing it. You go ahead and I'll stay here." He turned to look at me with a look that I had no choice. I realized if I held back, I would make a big scene, so I walked with him and felt like I was going to get sick or fall flat on my face.

Actually, I do a lot of praying and have had many seasons of deep intercessory prayer for people in great need, with some miraculous responses. And, being in front of people had *never* made me uncomfortable. I loved speaking to large groups. But praying up front?! So why was I opposed to pray for someone at church? I later realized that I was resisting what God had called me to do.

I finally made it to the front of the church, took a deep breath, and pulled out the tiny vile of anointing oil I carry in my purse. I was certain *no one* would come to us for prayer. They'd first go to one of the pastors.

Suddenly, I saw a lady coming directly towards us. I knew I had met her at Ladies Bible Study. My husband didn't know her, so he asked her name, and then asked how we could pray for her. Her name was Verna and she went on to share her great concern for her 5-year old twin grandsons. When she said they were anorexic, I was certain her information couldn't be possible because I had never heard of a child having this issue. She assured me it was true. Her husband, a doctor, confirmed it.

We talked for a minute and then I explained how I wanted to anoint her before we prayed. She was familiar with this because she had read about it several times in the Bible. I told her that she could stand in as a substitute for her 5-year old grandsons who were in Canada. She agreed.

Craig began to pray for her and I agreed in prayer with him. I suddenly felt the presence of Holy Spirit come over me and I began to cry. In my thoughts I felt like everyone who was left in the sanctuary was watching me and thinking I was crazy because the crying turned to grieving.

I knew what was happening. I had similar experiences at home when I went into fervent prayer. The Lord would often pour His Holy Spirit on me and I would respond in this same way, crying and doubled over with my stomach muscles so tight I couldn't straighten up.

I figured I'd better just trust the Lord with whatever He was doing with me because He never disappointed me when it happened before. It was God's way of telling me:

This is a serious matter and I don't want you in control when you pray. I want to take over.

That's exactly what happened. In the front of the church, all I could do was weep and in between sobs, say, "Jesus, heal these precious little boys, in the Name of Jesus!" Pretty simple prayer on my part.

Craig had prayed a prayer of faith and I was thinking mine was like a kindergarten prayer. I hadn't prayed any scriptures or even an eloquent prayer to give Verna hope, but she thanked us and we promised to pray throughout the week for these precious boys.

The next Sunday, as we stood in front, Verna came forward again. This time she brought a friend who was visiting. But first, she was eager to give us a report on her grandsons, telling us her daughter reported how the twins were doing much better. I was shocked! God had answered prayer, even in my fumbling. The boys continued to improve each week and we continued to pray for them until we finally learned they were doing amazingly well.

My faith soared.

On the next Sunday, I didn't care if I looked like a fool. God was doing the healing, not me. Verna introduced us to her friend who was deeply concerned for her good friend's adult daughter. She had a tumor in her brain. Now, I really felt inadequate, until I reminded the Lord that it was up to

Him to heal this woman's friend and to pray through my husband and me. So, I anointed the woman, standing in place for her dear friend, who also lived in Canada.

After we prayed, an unusual thought came to my mind. I said to the lady, "Do you have any anointing oil at home?" She didn't. So, I handed her mine. I encouraged her to anoint her friend on the forehead and say, "In the name of the Father, Son and Holy Spirit." Then, I encouraged her to lay her hand on the area of the brain where the tumor was, and pray for her healing. We wanted the tumor to shrink.

I also encouraged her to take some time to research healing scriptures in the Bible and ask her friend to read them to build up her faith. I assured her that we would be praying daily for her friend.

Weeks later, we learned the tumor was shrinking! All I could do was rejoice at how faithful our God is!

Then, a couple weeks later, I learned Verna had a heart attack! After days in the hospital, her family flew her back to Canada, even though they were concerned about her surviving the plane ride. Those of us who knew her, fervently began praying and believing for her healing.

Once again, God answered our prayers. It was such an amazing season to walk through. I didn't want these experiences to end.

Weeks later, I was thrilled to receive her report of good health. However, my heart was grieved to learn about her desperate prayer request for her 14-year-old granddaughter who had been cutting herself and trying to commit suicide! After reading her text, I immediately responded that I would go straight to prayer.

As before, I was overwhelmed with grieving. I knew the Lord was calling me to drop everything and fervently cry out to Him on this child's behalf.

As I wept before my Lord, I felt her granddaughter's pain of rejection at school and her young confused mind. She was wanting to be loved and understood. Her parent's love was there for her, but because of her insecurities, it didn't seem to be enough.

In time, I received a text from this girl's mother, the daughter of Verna. We had never met, but Verna had told her about my heart to pray for her daughter. The Lord opened the door to walk with this mother through her pain and deep concern for her child.

One day as I was praying, the Lord spoke into my spirit. He said, "Tell them to stop praying!" I was certain I had not heard correctly so I asked, "Lord, did you really tell me to tell them to stop praying?" I heard His response, "Tell them to start *Praising Me* for her daughter's healing."

I had learned years before the importance of the power in praise, but when a situation is really bad, we tend to beg the Lord for the person to be healed. I knew that *Praising Him, brings us to a place of full trust that He is in control.*

Thankfully, the family listened and they all began praising Him for what He was going to do. They began thanking Him for the miracle, even before it took place.

One day I received a call from Verna. She was excited to report that the mother had talked to her daughter, once again, about her cutting. After several moments, the child surrendered and prayed with her mother to give her life to Jesus. The cutting issue stopped completely. God had done it all!

God continued to be faithful, giving us more opportunities to serve in the prayer ministry.

Then, one Sunday after praying in front, I headed to the back of the church. I noticed a young woman sitting towards the back. She was alone. I had no plans to stop because I was tired and hungry and wanted to return home. But I suddenly stopped in front of her. In my thoughts, I was thinking, *Lord, what are you doing?* My mouth opened and I said, "My husband and I just finished praying up front, and I wonder if *you* have any needs for prayer?" Her eyes began to water and my spirit knew something was wrong.

Awkwardly, I climbed over her and sat beside her, putting my arm on the back of her chair. By this time, she was crying hard, so I began to pray, "Jesus I don't know this lady's need but you do. I ask that…" Now I started crying with her and couldn't pray. In a few moments, we both settled down and I continued, "I ask You to meet her heart's desire and comfort her, in the name of Jesus."

She calmed down and shared her story. Her husband had been accused of a serious crime and could possibly go to prison. "We will know on Wednesday what will take place," she sobbed out her words.

With strong faith rising up in my spirit, I said, "My husband and I are going to be supporting you in prayer this week. We are going to ask for a miracle!" As she shared more, I learned that her husband had been wrongly accused and they had very little hope. It looked impossible that he would be acquitted. I gave her my phone number and name, and she promised she would let me know the verdict.

My heart ached for her and her husband. It was a very desperate matter and Craig and I took it seriously. Day and night, we took their situation to prayer and finally on Wednesday afternoon, the phone rang.

When I answered, I wasn't thinking of this young woman. My thoughts were on other things, so when I put the phone to my ear and said, "Hello," all I could hear was a woman crying. Once again, I said, "Hello?" I could hear the lady trying to speak and I finally realized who it was.

I soon discovered that her tears were tears of joy! God had answered our prayer and her husband had been acquitted. He was completely FREE! I rejoiced with her, crying and praising God for His faithfulness.

Yes, when we were first asked to stand in front of the sanctuary to pray for others, I had to learn that these Divine Appointments were all about Him.

He used me to partner with Him and my husband, even though I felt unworthy. All I needed to do was *surrender my will to Him and then...HE TOOK OVER.*

IMPACT of WRONG CHOICES

They too have a soul and need the Savior's love.

I realize these following 5 stories may seem a bit unusual, compared to the previous stories I've shared. However, I felt they needed to be separated into a section all their own; thus, the reason for them being placed towards the end.

When God introduced me to Rebecca's story through a dear friend, I immediately sensed God calling me to be part of her troubled life.

But I had no idea how *intense* my involvement would become. Then, when He asked me to do spiritual battle on her behalf, I began to see the many lost girls on the streets, like her, in a whole different light.

When we talk about issues like this, they are sometimes difficult to understand. It seems easier to bury our heads in the sand and not get involved.

For example, if we think about young women who get caught up in the sex industry, we may feel an aversion to them, or desire to avoid them entirely. However, *they too have a soul and need the Savior's love.*

God wants to extend His love to them through His people. It begins with allowing Him to place a caring spirit in each of our hearts. Then, to ask Him if we are to be involved in some way.

For me, He led me into a depth of prayer for Rebecca that I never would have imagined possible. Emotionally, I felt *on call* daily, to be available and willing whenever God spoke into my spirit and called me to do spiritual battle for her; it was often in the middle of the night.

You may never have heard of people having spiritual *visions* or *praying in the Spirit*, as explained in the Book of Acts of the Bible. However, I was walking in unfamiliar territory and never could have walked through this season without the Holy Spirit's leading and training me how to respond and how to pray.

These troubled young women may appear confident but they desperately long to escape the web of destruction Satan lured them into. Their hearts long to be free. They *need t*o know the Lord.

My desire is that, as you read Rebecca's stories, your heart will be touched and open to God's leading to pray for the *ladies of the night* in your own city.

ONE WOMAN'S STRUGGLE

*The Breath of God gently whispered
her name...REBECCA.*

She was in her late 20's when I learned of her turbulent life. I never had the opportunity to meet her in person, however, the Holy Spirit placed a deep desire for me to intercede in prayer for her.

I learned that Rebecca's birthmother was an alcoholic and prostitute. When her mother turned 16, Rebecca was born. Because of the birth mother's immaturity, and God's intervention, Rebecca was given to a stable Christian family when she was 5-months old. Her adoptive mother made certain that she taught Rebecca all the things she needed to know about life, and God's amazing love for her.

Rebecca came to love Jesus and gave her life to Him at an early age. In time, she was even baptized.

However, her birth mother's generational sins of dependence on alcohol, a life of wild and daring choices, and her involvement in prostitution, influenced Rebecca's strong personality. Her mind operated differently than most children and her thoughts became more twisted as she grew older.

The adoptive mother later learned that men had been watching and talking to her daughter through the fence at her middle-school playground. Without Rebecca even realizing it, these deceptive men were preparing her to someday meet her pimp. She was also introduced to alcohol, which she struggled with for the remainder of her life.

No matter how much love was poured into her life, the lure of large amounts of money enticed her into prostitution. Actually, she didn't want to live that kind of lifestyle, but she couldn't break free from the hold it had on her.

In time, she was introduced to a nice young man from a wonderful Christian family. But, due to poor choices they each made, a pregnancy soon resulted. Thankfully, she chose *not* to abort the pregnancy.

Rebecca loved her precious baby girl but found it difficult to care for her because of her late nights and wrong choices. In time, the couple separated.

Throughout her baby's life, the child often stayed with the father's parents. As their granddaughter grew older, both sets of grandparents saw the severity of issues in Rebecca's life, and they knew they needed to do something to help more consistently with their grandchild.

When the little girl was almost 8 years of age, the father's parents were granted custody. For way too long, they had painfully observed Rebecca's lifestyle, and were overjoyed to have the opportunity to lovingly care for their grandchild.

They knew it would not be easy to raise this precious child in their senior years, but they had great hope to influence and train her *in the way she should go* and trust that God would help her become the young woman He had created her to be.

I can't explain why God had placed Rebecca so deeply on my heart. There were times when I prayed for her such that my heart just ached to the core. The deep sobbing I often experienced during prayer could not be explained. I just knew God had called me to pray, and most of the time I felt like I was warring against the enemy of her soul!

This intense time of prayer went on for several weeks. Then one day, at 2:30 am, I woke up and could not return to sleep. Instead, *I felt the breath of God gently whisper her name…Rebecca.*

I sensed the Lord was doing something in the spiritual realm, and I had better get out of bed for a middle-of-the-night assignment.

As I prayed, I felt an anger building in me. The enemy was fighting to keep her locked into her addiction of alcohol and prostitution.

Rehabilitation was no match for the demonic hold on her life. She needed spiritual deliverance! Only God could deliver her from the pit of temptation and despair in which the enemy held her captive. My prayer partners & I had already been doing *warfare battle* for a long season; it appeared it was not going to end any time soon.

Several nights later as I was lying in bed, singing in my thoughts, and wishing I could return to sleep, an old hymn I had sung as a young girl came to mind.

> *Blessed assurance, Jesus is mine. Oh, what a foretaste of glory divine. Heir of Salvation, purchased of God. Born of His Spirit, washed in His blood. This is my story; this is my song. Praising my Savior, all the day long. This is my story; this is my song. Praising my Savior, all the day long.*

Over and over, I continued to sing this old hymn in my thoughts. I wanted to sing loudly and worship my Lord, even if it was the middle of the night. However, my husband was sleeping.

I had been praying for Rebecca and wondered what this song had to do with her. Then, the Lord showed me that when she surrendered her life to Him, she also would be singing His praises and sharing her story with many broken lives who were walking her same path.

I longed for a complete breakthrough in her life. Then I sensed the Lord encouraging me to pray for the men she was involved with over the years. They needed Jesus, too. I knew her breakthrough would have a profound impact on them.

I continued interceding in prayer for Rebecca for a long season.

Then, during one of the middle-of-the-night prayer times, I asked the Lord why He couldn't remind me during the day to pray for Rebecca; after all, I needed my rest! He gently responded, "You are too busy during the day and you tend to listen to Me more carefully during the night."

OK, Lord, I get the message.

NOTE: I continued to fervently pray for Rebecca and had no idea what more could possibly take place. Little did I know of the visions God would soon show me in my spirit. I was always humbled and amazed when they took place. The following stories, CALL TO BATTLE 1–4, are the experiences that continued to revolve around Rebecca's life.

CALL to BATTLE #1

*God uses us to wage war against
the enemy of a troubled soul.*

I t had been a late night. The annual 4th of July celebration finally ended with the massive display of fireworks over the lake. Our son and family, who were living with us at the time, would return home after the neighborhood settled down with its own fireworks.

My husband and I went to bed at 11pm and had no plans to rise until 7am.

However, at 1:45am, I was awakened for no obvious reason. I rationalized, *Lord, you couldn't want me to get up after less than three hours of sleep.* I didn't listen to His call and allowed myself to immediately fall back into a deep sleep.

Suddenly, only 15 minutes later, our security alarm sounded outside our bedroom. I couldn't figure out what was happening. The hall light turned on and I heard our adult son rushing down the stairs. I grabbed my bathrobe and ran out to the hallway. There stood my daughter-in-law and oldest grandson. She explained that our 9-year-old grandson had been sleep-walking, going down the stairs and heading out the front door. Our son caught him just in time.

As I headed back to bed, I thought, *Lord, there must be something really important that needs prayer or you wouldn't have allowed so much drama to get my attention!*

By this time, I was wide awake, so I went downstairs to pray. I asked, "OK Lord, who is it? Who needs prayer at this hour of the night?"

Suddenly, Rebecca, the young mother my friend had shared her concern about, came to mind. It was amazing how I had never met her, but I was certain God had chosen me to intercede for her in prayer!

As I began praying, the Holy Spirit gave me a vision of her in an exclusive hotel suite. I sensed the Holy Spirit encouraging me to call her by name, saying, *"Rebecca, come out!"* I repeated it several times. Tears began to flow, and once again, I felt the pull on her by an evil spirit. That's when I began to fight the enemy. I let him know he had no right to her life because my Lord was calling her out of *the pit of prostitution* and had a purpose for her life!

Over and over, I pounded my fist on my knees, showing him my authority as I spoke in the *Name of Jesus.* I was *not* going to give up the fight!

It was Saturday night and I knew it was her *work* night. However, by this time she would probably be sound asleep on the plush bed in their luxuriously-appointed room. I didn't want to think about the wealthy customer who shared her bed.

At this point, it wasn't about him; it was about her troubled life! I knew *Jesus was calling her back to Him.* She had loved Him since she was a young child.

Suddenly, the Bible story of young Samuel (I Samuel 3:4-20) came to mind. I remembered how a voice had awakened him when he was living with the priest, Eli. In the middle of the night, Samuel went to Eli and said, "Here I am; you called me?" Eli answered, "I did *not* call you, go back to sleep." This happened a second time; when it happened the third time, he went to Eli and the priest responded, "Go lie down, and if He calls you, say, "Speak, Lord for your servant is listening."

Because I couldn't call Rebecca, but I knew the Holy Spirit could, I began to pray, *"Holy Spirit, I ask you to awaken Rebecca. Call her by name until she remembers that Bible story and answers, "Speak Lord."*

I continued for some time, believing she heard her name being called. Did she answer? Only the Lord knows. All I know is… *I am to remain faithful and continue to listen in my spirit when He calls me to pray.*

No matter if it's day or night, I want to be sensitive to hear His call, and follow His leading – even if it takes a security alarm to get my attention.

Am I concerned about the nights when my sleep is interrupted and I don't receive the amount I feel I need? For years my sleep was more important than just about anything; I had suffered from Chronic Fatigue Syndrome and sleep was critical.

However, when I came to the place where...

I desired my relationship with the
Lord to become more intimate,
I even gave Him permission to awaken
me in the middle of the night.

If He wanted to meet with me, or if someone needed prayer, I wanted to be available.

This was an amazing turnaround because I *never* had a strong desire to be an intercessor. By making that decision, He began to teach me how critical this middle-of-the-night call to pray was.

I thought, *Lord, I'm going to rely on You to awaken me.* He heard me and quickly answered my prayer that very night. And, He has continued every night He has wanted to meet with me.

Actually, He uses some very unlikely sounds: my cell phone whistling (incoming texts)…the smoke alarm…my cell phone ringing…my name being called…the neighbor dog barking in our room…my husband snoring, etc.

Each time I awaken, our bedroom is silent. The Holy Spirit produces these crazy sounds for only my ears to hear. Many times, when He awakened me with these sounds, I'd get up and think, *Lord, you are so funny! I know you caused that sound! So, here I am. Who is in need of serious prayer that can't wait until morning?*

These days, I seldom question Him anymore. He now uses cramps in my feet, causing me to really spring out of bed!

There are always needs to be brought to the Throne of Grace. However, during the Rebecca season of praying, He called me to partner with Him, and hopefully others, to join with Him in warring against the enemy of her soul.

I felt strongly that He would bring her out of her painfully difficult lifestyle and her testimony would be victorious. I knew we could *not* give up the fight! However, the battle continued as you will see in CALL TO BATTLE #2–4.

CALL to BATTLE #2

Jesus, do in her what she can't do for herself.

I t was my birthday, and after a full day of activity, I was exhausted. At 11pm Craig and I had finally gone to bed. As always, we joined hands as we talked and prepared to pray. He wasn't feeling well so I led in prayer that evening.

Immediately, Rebecca came to mind.

As I began praying, a familiar grieving emotion rushed in and I knew the Holy Spirit was preparing to do something precious, but Satan was pulling for all he was worth, to undo what God wanted to accomplish. I also knew the Lord was calling me to stand in the gap for this young woman, even though we had never met.

A few nights earlier, she came to mind for the first time, as I experienced one of those middle-of-the-night sessions when the Lord awakens me and calls me to prayer.

It was *that* evening when I had a vision of *her sharing her testimony* on the streets with women who were standing around, waiting to be picked up by unknown men. She was bold, but tender, as she told the young prostitutes how she had left this painful lifestyle because Jesus had changed her life and He could change their lives also.

Now, for the second time, the Lord brought her to mind.

After my husband and I finished praying, I tried falling to sleep but Rebecca kept coming to mind. I didn't know what else to do but continue to pray.

Then, it happened again – another vision. My eyes were closed and I saw her wearing a loose-fitting long white linen skirt and a matching ¾ length smock top with loose sleeves and a collarless split tunic. It fit loosely over her skirt.

I was surprised to see this picture because the other visions I'd seen of people dressed like this, were people who had died and were in heaven.

I saw her hands raised and she was tenderly worshiping the Lord!

After these two experiences, I was convinced that God was planning on doing a transforming work in her life. I also knew there was going to be war in the spirit world; this had to be the reason why God was calling for such deep intercessory prayer.

Finally, around midnight, I fell asleep. However, at 2:30a.m. my sleep was interrupted by my husband, who was returning from the bathroom. Usually, I don't hear him but this time I decided to also use the restroom.

The Holy Spirit began to speak to me in this most unlikely place, and His message was clear. I knew I couldn't return to bed. Instead, I put on my bathrobe and quietly went downstairs to pray in the spirit for this young mother.

As I sat on the sofa to pray, these words came out of my mouth: "Jesus, You know where she is tonight. You know the tugging in her heart; the longing to run to You. But she's so locked into the vicious cycle of drugs, alcohol, and prostitution. She just can't break free on her own! Lord, you've got to provide a way. *Do in her what she can't do for herself.* I know she must hate this way of life because she comes from a godly heritage. I'm convinced she loves You, but she is bound and shackled with emotional chains. Free her Lord, through the power of your Holy Spirit! She needs YOU to provide the key to unlock the chains in her life… in Jesus Name!"

I continued praying in the Spirit and then, for the third time, another vision took place.

I sensed I was standing behind the Lord in what appeared to be a hotel room. He was standing next to a King Size bed where this young mother was sleeping. He reached down and touched her, and when she awoke, He did not speak, but she knew He was lovingly asking to take her hand so that He could lift her up. Without hesitation, she reached out to Him. As she was helped up, she was also being pulled in the opposite direction by an unseen force.

Gradually, the Lord brought her to Himself and as she stood, He wrapped His arms around her, and she placed her head on His chest.

Within moments, He was no longer there and I was left alone with her. I knew that her soul (mind, emotions, will & conscience) needed anointing. So, I symbolically took my anointing oil and placed it on her forehead and prayed. Slowly, she raised her hands and began to quietly worship.

I knew in my spirit that she longed to be free, but the old patterns of wrong choices were painfully difficult to leave. She couldn't let go.

I then began to speak "FREEDOM" into her mind, freedom for the chains to be broken and a desire for her to run from the sin that had claimed her soul and tied her into such deep bondage.

When the vision ended, I asked the Lord *why* He had given me these three visions about this *one* young woman.

Instantly, I knew the answer. It was because He had called me to intercede for her in prayer. I also knew I couldn't do it alone and would need the spiritual power of my *Fervent Five* Prayer Partners. It would take all of us to war in the spirit on Rebecca's behalf. She was too weak to leave her lifestyle. The enemy had fed her so many lies, one being that she couldn't continue to live extravagantly as she had been doing. The power of Satan had his claws in too deep!

I am sharing all of this to paint a clear picture of what was happening in the spirit with regards to this mother and all women who get hooked.

Perhaps you know someone who is bound by a sexual addiction of prostitution. If you don't personally know anyone in this category, would you be willing to join with me to do battle in the spirit for young women in your city who have lost their way and can't get out of this horrible addiction?

Would you be willing to be awakened in the middle of the night, if God calls you get up to pray? Remember, the late night is her *work time.* and she needs to be covered in prayer!

I truly believe that deep down inside, these women long to break free, but cannot. They need prayer warriors to stand in the gap on their behalf.

The amazing truth is that when a woman yields to Christ, her heart is going to be so radically changed that her entire life will be absolutely transformed! Our God can do much more than we could hope or ask. (based on Ephesians 3:20)

I believe our Lord is going to call Christian women all over the world to accomplish His purpose, as He restores one life at a time.

CALL to BATTLE #3

*I receive an amazing blessing when I partner
with Him on a spiritual assignment.*

It was 11:56 pm when I was awakened by the familiar whistle on my cellphone. I thought, *who in the world would be texting me this late at night?*

I didn't want to awaken my husband, so I quietly crawled out of bed to grab my phone before the 2nd notification sounded. I opened the cover and suddenly remembered I had turned my phone off before I went to bed.

Once again, the sound did not actually come from my cell. It was the sound the Lord creates *only for my ears* to hear it in the middle of the night. He was calling me to intercessory prayer for a serious need. As I put on my bathrobe, I smiled, *OK, Lord, I know it's You! Isn't there anyone else you can awaken to pray?*

I smile after I ask such a silly question.

I was not upset. I was just curious. Certainly, there was someone else who could occasionally take the late-night assignment. Although I wanted my sleep to be uninterrupted, I also didn't want to miss what the Lord had waiting for me. Each time this happens, *I receive an amazing blessing when I partner with Him on a spiritual assignment.*

As I walked downstairs, I wondered who was in such desperate need that He would awaken me. I headed straight for the L-shaped sofa in the family room. I love sitting on the end where I can prop up my feet, add a blanket, a pillow behind my neck, and then relax by the fireplace as I begin to pray. I knew I had better get comfortable because I may be there for a while.

I started with praise and worship, thanking my precious Lord for allowing me to experience His presence. Then I thanked Him for trusting me to partner with Him for individuals who were in desperate spiritual or emotional need for healing.

Should I be surprised that within moments, Rebecca came to mind?

This was the third evening God had awakened me to pray for her. I thought, *things must be heating up in her life.*

Once again, just like the previous week, I realized it was midnight on Saturday, and she had possibly driven to the city where she did her *work*.

I knew the familiar routine, so I quickly began my conversation with the Lord. However, instead of praying for her, the Holy Spirit directed me to speak to her so-called lover! Making a fist and pointing at him as though he was standing directly in front of me, I shouted in a whisper (not to awaken the family), "STOP IT! STOP IT NOW, IN THE NAME OF JESUS!"

As I prayed, my eyes were covered with my cushy satin sleep mask to block out any distractions that the outside streetlight might show.

In the darkness, the Lord once again gave me *a vision* of a plush hotel room with its King size bed and white crisply ironed sheets. On the opposite wall, across from the bed, was an extra-large screen TV. I saw the shape of a man as he tried to convincingly speak to Rebecca.

I knew something was wrong when tears started to flow down my cheeks. My spirit was troubled. Soon I could see that he was trying to lure her to watch a video. She was trying to resist because it was a seductive video that she did not want to watch. "NOOOO! God, please take her out of this sexual abuse," I prayed.

My tears quickly turned to sobbing. I wanted to step into her environment, pull her out and take her far away. I felt the enemy's strong hold on her, and my heart ached and yearned to help her run. I kept crying out to her, "RUN, REBECCA, RUN!"

Suddenly, my thoughts turned to the possible wife of this man, who may be home with her family. He might have been single, but if he did have a wife, I asked the Lord to bring a Christian woman to minister the love of God to her.

If a wife exists, she knows something is wrong, even if he is covering all his tracks. Yet, she believes his lies. She may question her own thoughts, but she desperately wants to trust him. But deep down inside she knows something is not right.

I continued to carry the possible wife in prayer until the Lord took me in a different direction.

I was amazed how the Holy Spirit was directing me to pray specifically for what was needed. Now His focus returned to Rebecca.

I felt led to ask the Lord to bring memories to Rebecca about her childhood; memories of when she was taught by her godly adoptive mother about Jesus. I asked Him to bring Bible stories, scriptures, and spiritual truths that would tug at the deception and dissatisfaction within her. And then, to give her freedom to flee her lucrative lifestyle.

At one point, through my sobbing tears, I said, "Lord, I know you can do this on your own, but thank You for asking me to partner with You. I am not a mighty prayer warrior like some of my close prayer partners. They speak with authority, using scripture and eloquent words. I am so simple with my words. But Lord, if you can, please use me. I'm willing to be obedient when you call me to war in the spirit."

I continued, "Jesus, fight for her…she's so weak."

I wasn't feeling a specific direction to pray so I began to pray through His spirit, with my sobbing tears. I was certain He heard and was answering my heart's cry.

My heart continued to grieve for her as I felt anger and disgust regarding the man in her life. However, the Lord spoke to my spirit telling me that He too had a soul. I didn't want to think about this possibility. I just wanted to stay on her side and hold the anger I had towards him. Yet somehow, I knew this man was trying to fill the deep emptiness in his heart. His depraved mind didn't realize he was turning to the wrong things to fill his life.

Soon, I felt led to pray for his soul.

As he stood before me, in my thoughts, I started with his mind. In the spirit, I placed my hands on his head, and began speaking against the demonic control over his mind. I prayed that he would choose to fight the strong desire to have Rebecca in his life, and for his eyes to be opened to see her as a precious, pure woman. I prayed that he would have compassion and gently tell her they needed to stop meeting.

My thoughts returned to the scene where the man was trying to get Rebecca to watch the video. For no apparent reason, the video had stopped working. He sensed his grandmother had been praying because the torment in his life was becoming more intense. He shared with Rebecca what was happening. She told him she was feeling the same way. They realized they each needed to make an escape; they *had* to separate! They could not handle the pressure anymore.

The hounds of heaven were after them.

He felt like he was going crazy! He had lived a double life way too long, and *he hated himself for it.* The depression and turmoil were swallowing him up.

I heard Rebecca say, "What am I going to do?" Jesus spoke to her spirit, tenderly. *"Trust me, Rebecca. I love you."*

Trust was difficult for Rebecca. She didn't know if she could trust what she thought she heard Him say. She had ignored His voice for so many years and she wondered if it was really His voice. Then, the scene I had been watching in the vision, came to a close.

It all seemed so amazing how the Holy Spirit had allowed me to see this vision!

All I could do was sit and worship the Lord for what He was doing in the life of Rebecca, and those other individuals associated with her mixed-up life. I even prayed the Lord would give her a testimony when she came out of this pit, a testimony of His *Amazing Grace.*

I could hear the words being sung from the old timeless hymn. It was the one He would use in both of their lives as their blinded eyes were opened.

Two hours later I was still lingering in God's Presence until I felt His peace. I then returned to bed. Sleep came quickly as I fell into the arms of my loving Savior.

The next morning, I was pondering how the Lord was giving me physical strength for this new day, even after that long night. It was as though I had slept through the entire night without interruption! Only God could do this for me.

I know, beyond a shadow of doubt, God is working in Rebecca's life. *She will* come out of this tormenting lifestyle! *She will* have an amazing story to share with those who struggle with her same addictions.

The words to the song "Amazing Grace" *will* have new meaning in her life. And, s*he will not* pass her addictions of drugs, alcohol, and sexual addiction to the next generation!

> *"Amazing Grace, how sweet the sound,*
> *that saved a wretch like me.*
> *I once was lost, but now I'm found;*
> *was blind, but now I see!"*

CALL to BATTLE #4

We can choose who we will follow.
(based on Joshua 24:15)

I t was a day of crazy happenings – certainly not one that cooperated with our plans for that Saturday.

It started with a call from our adult son. He and his family were returning from a week at Glacier National Park and made it to a quaint little town that was seven hours away from their home.

They abruptly stopped when their four-wheel-drive vehicle broke down. There was only one little log cabin style motel in this unique little Idaho town. Thankfully there was a shop that could work on the car; but the mechanic was unable to find the problem.

That's when we received the call for help.

Telephone calls were exchanged back and forth, examining every possibility to getting them home.

Finally, the decision was made. My husband borrowed our relative's vehicle with a tow bar. He would drive to their destination, but it would mean a 14-hour round-trip. All went well. Praise God they made it home safely by 2:30 a.m.

While I waited, I had plenty of projects to keep me busy.

It started with a morning where I ministered to a 49-year-old woman for three hours in my home. She had come to mind several times, which surprised me. I hadn't seen her for two to three years. I assumed the Lord had a purpose in mind, and after she started sharing all her issues, I began to understand what He was doing. He was so faithful to give wisdom in sharing hope for this hopeless situation she was dealing with.

I then knew this was why I didn't have peace about going on the trip to "rescue" our kids.

Then I was busy all day with house work, emails, and texts to encourage those who contacted me. Late that evening I considered heading to bed; however, I felt the Lord encouraging me to stay up and wait for my family to return.

I knew I could use that time to do spiritual battle for the woman I had met with earlier that day. But instead, Rebecca came to mind.

I thought, *of course, it's Saturday night, her work night!* For the past month, the Holy Spirit had clearly brought her to my mind for prayer every Saturday night. I knew I couldn't just give a simple little prayer on her behalf. Her situation always ended up being a real *Call to Battle*.

I learned she had been showing a lot of antagonism towards her child's father and his parents. These were the grandparents who lavished their love on her, even in the midst of her shady lifestyle.

This negative attitude on her part made me realize even more that the enemy of her soul was fighting to keep her in bondage.

One side of her deeply longed to get out of this hellish lifestyle, while the other side enjoyed the affluent financial consistency it provided.

The truth is, she couldn't get out, even if she wanted to leave! The enemy's claws were in too deep and she knew it. Between her negative and angry conversations with her child's grandmother, she surprisingly revealed the visions the Lord gave her when she was in High School, shortly after she yielded to the pimp who drew her into this demoralizing way of life.

She knew God had His hand on her life…but after she tasted the financial freedom, and the more deeply her rebellious lifestyle became – she knew Satan's powerful hold would not release her.

The thought of this distasteful web of shame broke my heart and motivated me to pray even more.

That night as I prayed, I didn't have another vision, but I clearly began to understand there was only one way the enemy would lose his grip on her life!

All along, I had prayed the Lord would bring her out of the pit she was in, but I began to realize that's *not* always how He works.

God gives us the freedom to make choices, good or bad ones.

Although He is more powerful than Satan and could easily remove her from her destructive lifestyle, *He often waits for us to make the choice* – a choice to trust Him with our life, with an opportunity to yield our heart to Him!

When this realization came, I began to firmly speak to her through the spirit, like I had done so many times before.

I said…

"Rebecca, you have got to make a choice! Even God's Word says, *choose you this day whom you will follow*! [based on Joshua 24:15]

"It also says, *trust in the Lord with all your heart.* [based on Proverbs 3:5] It means to STOP leaning on your own understanding, as to how you think you can't live without your lucrative income; you are believing a lie! Don't you realize that God could take that away from you in a heartbeat? Plus, He is quite capable to financially take care of you. All you need to do is allow HIM to take over your life and provide for you. TRUST HIM!"

I didn't experience the usual emotion that came with my spiritual interaction concerning her, but I knew the Holy Spirit was using my simple prayer to tug at her heart. I sensed this spiritual battle was going to be a difficult one. She had allowed her poor choices to go on for too many years and Satan's hold on her was severely entrenched. Only JESUS could bring her out of this way of living.

But *she* had to make the *choice* to turn to Him! He had given her a free will to choose Satan's lies or Jesus, Who is the Way, the Truth, and the Life." (John 14:6)

UPDATE: There were many more CALLS TO BATTLE prayer times for Rebecca, but I didn't record them. She was the Holy Spirit's regular choice during my prayer vigils.

Sometime later I heard the shocking news that she was missing!

I felt the stab in my heart and couldn't believe it was true. I had been believing for the miracle of her coming out of the horrible life she was living! I know all this might seem unusual, though I had never met her in person. But God had given me a deep heart of compassion and motherly concern for Rebecca's well-being.

I can't explain it. I just knew God had asked me to *partner* with Him, for her.

Months later, the long search had come to an end. I learned the authorities had labeled the case as a homicide! Wouldn't you think I'd be falling apart? Instead, there was a *peace in my heart.*

I COULDN'T EXPLAIN IT. . .
I FELT SHE WAS WITH JESUS!

After the life she lived, was that really possible? Would God take her home to be with Him for eternity?

I believe God knew that in Rebecca's case, the only way her cycle of bondage could be broken would be if He allowed her life to be taken. And, as she was passing from this earth, Jesus instantly appeared to her and she surrendered to Him.

Did He forgive her? Yes, I believe He did, and then He carried her home to Heaven!

How can I believe this to be true? First, when I learned the news, I felt such an incredible peace in my spirit. And secondly, as I prayed about her, I felt God whisper in my spirit, *your job is done. She is now with Me.*

In years past, I would have had a difficult time believing this was even possible, but after I read a book about Near Death Experiences (people who had died and come back), I heard stories about people who had no relationship with Jesus, but as they were beginning to pass into eternity, Jesus appeared to them. In each recorded story when they saw Jesus, they chose to follow Him. Some He sent back to earth to tell their story. In those situations, they followed Jesus for the remainder of their lives.

I know Rebecca loved Jesus until the end of her life, but she could not break the bondages in her own strength. She needed Him.

I truly believe Rebecca's struggle is now over. She is free of her earthly addictions. She is wearing a white linen garment like I have seen in my visions. She is singing praises to Jesus whom she grew to love as a little girl. Satan stole her life as a teenager, but in the end, God redeemed it for Himself. She surrendered to Him as she walked into eternity!

Yes, He won the victory over Satan and we, too, can experience His victory in our lives.

1 Corinthians 15:57 NKJV even shares this truth: "But thanks be to God, who gives *us* the victory through our Lord Jesus Christ."

THE BLESSING

The Lord bless you and keep you.

I once heard a lady speak to a MOPS group (Mothers of Preschoolers), where I was a mentor. She shared an experience that related to an Old Testament portion of scripture found in Numbers 6:24-26. After she put it to memory, God used it to bless her fussy granddaughter in a most unusual way.

I was intrigued by this life-lesson but had no expectation I would ever be using it with my own grandchildren. Actually, the reason I decided to put it to memory was because I thought it was a great blessing to share with others. Then, after I memorized it, I didn't give it much thought.

Months later, I received a call from our son, Gregory, asking if I would consider coming to Washington D.C.

He and Christy needed a babysitter for our 19-month-old grandson, only for a couple days while he and our daughter-in-law attended a short conference. I was thrilled to be asked.

When the departure date arrived, I took the 5-hour-flight and landed late that afternoon before dinner. I was grateful it gave me time to reacquaint and interact with our grandson. At bedtime, my daughter-in-law suggested I put Jack to bed so I could learn his bedtime routine, before they left. "It is simple," she explained, "As long as he has his little blue blanket, he will go right to sleep."

The next morning, following breakfast, mommy & daddy left for their conference and I pulled out the toys to entertain Jack. He was our first grandchild and it had been years since I had cared for one so young. Thankfully, he seemed to be doing okay with his Nana's care.

After lunch, I followed Christy's list of instructions and put him to bed for his afternoon nap. I remembered that all I had to do was give him his favorite silky blue blanket and leave the room.

It turned out it wasn't that easy!

The moment I placed him in his bed and turned around to leave, he stood up and began to cry! I quickly laid him down, reminding him it was time to go sleepy-night-night, but it simply didn't work.

What was I doing wrong?! His crying persisted so I picked him up and comforted him. When he finally stopped crying, I gently placed him back in his crib. However, as I quietly left his bedroom, he stood up and immediately began to cry again… loudly!

The Blessing

I thought, *why isn't this working?*

I returned to his bed and tried lying him down again but the crying only got louder and uncontrolled. Once again, I picked him up and this time it took extra time to quiet him down.

I started all over by giving him his favorite blue blanket, speaking loving words to him, kissing him good night, placing him back in his bed, and quietly walking out of his bedroom. Once again, it did not work! He knew mommy and daddy were gone and that's who he wanted.

As I stood next to the wall in the hallway, I covered my face with my hands, softly praying, *"Lord, help me! I don't know what else to do to quiet him. Should I just let him cry himself to sleep?"* His crying now sounded mournful and I was certain big crocodile tears were saturating his face. Then I said, *"Jesus, I can't do this but You can; please do it through me."*

Suddenly, the memory of that speaker's experience, from months earlier, came flooding into my thoughts. I still remembered the Numbers 6:24-26 blessing, so I returned to his room.

First, I picked him up and tenderly quieted him and then gently laid him down with his little blue blanket. However, *this time* I immediately placed my hand on his forehead, softly saying:

The Lord bless you and keep you; the Lord make his face shine upon you and be gracious unto you; the Lord lift up His countenance upon you and give you peace. Amen. (Numbers 6:24-26 NKJV)

As I said these words, my mind was thinking, *He doesn't have a clue what I'm saying.*

Yet, to my surprise and delight, it worked! He kept absolutely silent as long as my hand was on his forehead and I was praying the blessing.

The moment I lifted my hand, he began to cry. It took three times. When I finished the third time and lifted my hand, he remained quiet. I was delighted and figured he finally gave up and was probably thinking: *This Nana of mine is never going to stop saying all those words so I might as well go to sleep.*

That night, at bedtime, I placed him in his bed and before he even had a chance to whimper, I quickly placed my hand on his forehead and began praying the same blessing.

However, when I lifted my hand, he began to fuss. I did it a second time and suddenly he was silent. I was encouraged. It only took two blessings that night.

The next day, for the 3rd bed-time experience, it only took one time to say the blessing and he went to sleep! From then on, it continued to work. Matter-of-fact, whenever I

The Blessing

placed him in bed, he'd look up at me and smile, as though he was saying, *Nana, aren't you going to bless me?*

When it was time for me to return to Seattle, our son and Jack drove me to the airport. It was going to be difficult leaving him, but I made certain I took a moment and blessed him one last time before I kissed him goodbye.

A few days later, I missed him terribly, so I called Christy. She was sitting at the table feeding Jack his last bite of breakfast. I asked, "Will you put me on your speaker phone so I can talk to Jack?" When I knew he was listening, I reminded him that I was Nana and I flew back to my home on a big airplane. After a little more chit chat, of which he gave no answer except to point at the phone, I said, "Nana wants to give you 'The Blessing.'" I then asked Christy to put her hand on his forehead while I prayed the same blessing he had heard when I visited.

I began the words and after he heard the last word, *peace*, he said, "Aw-mun" at the exact second, I said, "Amen." Hearing his sweet voice was such a joy.

Afterwards, Christy told me Jack had done something interesting when I was praying the blessing. She had reached out her hand towards him but he obviously didn't think she was doing it correctly so he pulled her hand close to his forehead and leaned forward, while he held it in place until I finished.

I explained, "He probably did that because that's what I did when I put him to bed each time and prayed the blessing over him!

When Jack and then his brother, Samuel, joined the family, each time I was with them, I gave them the *blessing* at night before they went to sleep. As they grew older, *they* insisted on blessing me as well.

So, I got a double portion gift as each child individually placed his hand on my forehead and began to say the words, "The Lord bless you and keep you…" I was thrilled when they quoted it in entirety.

Young moms have told me that *the blessing* even works if a child is feeling unsettled, agitated, or frustrated. I was thrilled to hear the benefits of this amazing blessing from God's Word.

One day I was thinking about those few verses and the impact they had on both the speaker's granddaughter and my grandsons.

> *God's Word is always true and it breathes life*
> *through His Holy Spirit to people of all ages.*

DON'T GIVE UP

God doesn't call the equipped,
He equips the called.

The following story was one I had saved after I discovered it in one of those boxes that got moved with us to our current home, but never got cleaned out and tossed.

I am embarrassed to say that there was stuff in that box I had not seen for *over* ten years. However, as I read it, it seemed that it was given to me by God in His perfect timing!

He knew how many times I wanted to give up writing this book, but I knew it was His assignment for me.

As I started throwing old papers from the box, I sensed the tattered paper in my hand was meant for me to read. This is what it said:

> "Wishing to encourage her young son's progress on the piano, a mother took the small boy to a Paderewski concert. After they were seated, the mother spotted a friend in the audience and walked down the aisle to greet her. Seizing the opportunity to explore the wonders of the concert

hall, the little boy rose and eventually explored his way through a door marked: NO ADMITTANCE.

"Then, when the house lights suddenly dimmed, the curtains parted and spotlights focused on the impressive Steinway on the stage. In horror, the mother saw her little boy sitting at the keyboard, innocently picking out, 'Twinkle, Twinkle Little Star.'

"At that moment, the great piano master made his entrance and quickly moved to the piano. He leaned down and whispered in the boy's ear, 'Don't quit. Keep playing.' Then leaning over, Paderewski reached down with his left hand and began filling in a bass part. Soon his right arm reached around to the other side of the child and he added a running *obligato*.

"Together, the old master and the young novice transformed a frightening situation into a wonderfully creative experience! The audience was mesmerized.

"That's the way it is with God. What we can accomplish on our own is hardly noteworthy. We try our best, but the results aren't exactly graceful flowing music. But with the hand of the Master, our life's work truly can be beautiful.

"Next time you set out to accomplish great feats, listen carefully. You can hear the voice of the Master, whispering in your ear. 'Don't quit. Keep playing.' And as we do, He augments and supplements, until work of amazing beauty is created.

"Feel His loving arms around you. Know what His strong hands are playing the concerto of your life." (Author Unknown)

As I read this precious story, tears blurred my vision. That story was meant for me!

How about you? Has God asked you to do something and you responded, "I can't," because it looked impossible and you gave up? That was my story. It took *years* before I surrendered.

Then, one day my husband said, "Karen, do you know how to eat an elephant?" I had never heard that question before. I thought it was a joke, until he answered his own question, "One bite at a time."

I got the message and knew I couldn't finish writing this book until I took the first bite.

I bowed my head and asked the Lord to write it through me. And, as I started writing, I sensed the surge of His

Spirit surge through me – and after that, I didn't want to stop writing!

That's how <u>DIVINE LOVE on Assignment</u> began.

***Don't Give Up! God has a purpose
for what He has asked of you!***

FINAL THOUGHTS

I am so grateful you invested your time in reading this book. Have you ever experienced a true story that was clearly a Divine Appointment, one that only God could have orchestrated? If so, I encourage you to write it out and save it. You may have an opportunity to share it someday.

Then, be open to notice how God is actually involved in these kinds of experiences. Does this lead you to look at everyday encounters differently...it sure does me!

Once again, my prayer is that you have been blessed by these stories and you will long to know God in a deeper way. I know He loves you and desires to grow closer to you!

Karen

The important lesson for me…
is to always be obedient to what
the Lord asks of me.

SCRIPTURE REFERENCES

PRODUCER OF STAR WARS

1 Peter 3:15b *"Always be prepared to give an answer to everyone who asks you to give the reason for the hope that you have. But do this with gentleness and respect."* (NIV)

Isaiah 50:4 *"The Sovereign Lord has given me His words of wisdom, so that I know how to comfort the weary. Morning by morning He wakens me and opens my understanding to His will."* (NLT)

BAG OF POTATOES

Matthew 6:33 *"But seek first His kingdom and His righteousness and all these things will be given to you..."* (NIV)

MY WHITE HAIR

1 John 1:9 *"If we confess our sins, He is faithful and just and will forgive us our sins and purify us from all unrighteousness.* (NIV)

Micah 7:19 *"You will again have compassion on us; you will tread our sins underfoot and hurl all our iniquities into the depths of the sea."* (NIV)

John 3:16 *"For God so loved the world that He gave His one and only Son, that whoever believes in Him shall not perish but have eternal life."* (NIV)

Romans 8:1 *"Therefore, there is now no condemnation for those who are in Christ Jesus."* (NIV)

ASPEN WITH NO HORSERADISH

Roman's 8:1 and John 3:16 are quoted in the above story.

Psalm 51:7 *"Purify me from my sins, and I will be clean; wash me and I will be whiter than snow."* (NLT)

HIS STORY CONTINUES

Proverbs 18:21a *"The tongue has the power of life and death..."* (NIV)

James 1:6-8 *"But when you ask, you must believe and not doubt, because the one who doubts is like a wave of the sea, blown and tossed by the wind. That person should not expect to receive anything from the Lord. Such a person is double-minded and unstable in all they do."* (NIV)

SHE NODDED

Jeremiah 29:11 *"For I know the plans I have for you,"* declares the Lord, *"plans to prosper you and not harm you, plans to give you hope and a future."* (NIV)

SURE WASN'T MY PLAN

Ezekiel 37:1 *"The Lord took hold of me, and I was carried away by the Spirit of the Lord ..."* (NLT)

I'M EVERYWHERE

Matthew 25:35-36,40 *"For I was hungry and you gave me something to eat, I was thirsty and you gave me something to drink, I was a stranger and you invited me in, I needed clothes and you clothed me, I was sick and you looked after me, I was in prison and you came to visit me..."* *"Truly I tell you, whatever you did for one of the least of these brothers and sisters of mine, you did it for me."* (NIV)

CALL TO BATTLE #1

1 Samuel 3:4-20 (shortened) *"The Lord called Samuel. Samuel answered, 'Here I am.' And he ran to Eli and said, 'Here I am; you called me.' But Eli said, 'I did not call; go back and lie down'... Eli realized that the Lord was calling the boy. So Eli told Samuel, 'Go and lie down, and if He calls you, say, 'Speak, Lord, for your servant is listening.'* (After the 3rd call...) *Then Samuel said, 'Speak, for your servant is listening'"* (NIV)

CALL TO BATTLE #2

Ephesians 3:20 *"Now to Him who is able to do immeasurably more than all we ask or imagine, according to His power that is at work within us."* (NIV)

CALL TO BATTLE #4

Joshua 24:15 *"Choose you this day whom you will serve… But as for me and my household, we will serve the Lord."* (NIV)

1 Corinthians 5:57 *"But thanks be to God, who gives us the victory through our Lord Christ Jesus."* (NIV)

THE BLESSING

Numbers 6:24-26 *"The Lord bless you and keep you; the Lord make His face shine upon you, and be gracious to you; the Lord lift up His countenance upon you and give you peace."* (NKJV)

KAREN and CRAIG KORTHASE

The picture on the right was taken by Alyssa Richardson, owner
of Divine One Studio. Any photo touch-up was also done by
her. She and her family live in Vancouver, WA.

KAREN LACOUNT KORTHASE

 Karen grew up the youngest of six children with an age range of 22 years.

God chose her older parents to shape her life in preparation for the gifting He would later use in her life.

After high school, she received her college degrees in Education and Music. It was in those late teenage formative years, she learned to listen to God's still small voice in her spirit and to stand firm in her faith, not following the crowd.

Karen loves sharing her love for Jesus and has had speaking engagements throughout Washington state, where she often shared her story of hope, after her first husband was killed in the Vietnam War.

Four years later, she met Craig when she left teaching and took a position as a Resident Director at Seattle Pacific University. They were later married.

And now, 50 years later, they are retired in Palm Springs, California, where they are involved in the community and their church, Desert Chapel. They have one son, his wife and two teen-age grandsons.

Karen is following God's prompting and will contribute all proceeds of this book to ministries that are reaching out to children who are suffering from Human Trafficking.